C000170814

OUR
LAND
AT WAR

OUR LAND AT WAR

BRITAIN'S KEY
FIRST WORLD WAR SITES

NICK BOSANQUET

All images are from the author's collection

First published 2014
by Spellmount, an imprint of

The History Press
The Mill, Brimscombe Port
Stroud, Gloucestershire, GL5 2QG
www.thehistorypress.co.uk

© Nick Bosanquet, 2014

The right of Nick Bosanquet to be identified as the Author
of this work has been asserted in accordance with the
Copyright, Designs and Patents Act 1988.

All rights reserved. No part of this book may be reprinted
or reproduced or utilised in any form or by any electronic,
mechanical or other means, now known or hereafter invented,
including photocopying and recording, or in any information
storage or retrieval system, without the permission in writing
from the Publishers.

British Library Cataloguing in Publication Data.
A catalogue record for this book is available from the British
Library.

ISBN 978 0 7524 9962 8

Typesetting and origination by The History Press
Printed in Great Britain

Contents

Acknowledgements

I acknowledge a considerable debt to the recent volume *With Our Backs to the Wall: Victory and Defeat in 1918* by Professor David Stevenson. This presents a balanced picture of the achievements as well as the tragedies and is a milestone in writing about the First World War. Special thanks to Adrian Denney for his help with the text and illustrations; to Jo DeVries and Rebecca Newton, editors at The History Press who have been most supportive; to Khuong To for his help with photographs; to Paul Stamper, Wayne Cocroft and Nicky Hughes of English Heritage for their help and encouragement; to Tara Finn on the search for Room 40; to Carole Harrington in Scarborough; and to Emily Mayhew for wise advice.

Introduction

The First World War was a challenge to a generation of Britons. Unexpected, not of their own making: at first a dark, threatening shadow over remote areas such as the seas off Chile, then closing into every street and family in the nation.

There is a compelling image of the war: soldiers in the mud on the Western Front across Belgium and France. But this is only one part of the story. Even for the British Army on the Western Front, by 1918 only 450,000 of the 1.4 million troops serving there were infantry, and even these infantry were no longer in fixed trench lines. Many more were in artillery, supplies and the Royal Air Force (RAF) in a new kind of machine war. Further back from the trenches the war created a war zone that took in most of the UK. This was the wider Western Front. Every town and every street was linked to the front line through service and through contribution to the war of the guns. The war mobilised not just soldiers but women workers, teenagers and even school children, who contributed their pennies to the war loans, picked fruit in summer and pushed sacks of coal in winter. Unlike the Second World War, which was fought a long way from home, the front line of the First World War was very close to home, a shadow on every coast and in the skies over the UK.

In this book we trace the main sites for this wider war effort – which can be found mostly in the UK – but to these we should add the hubs of Queenstown (Cobh) in Ireland and Calais in France. For a generation it was an unavoidable challenge that turned into a 'test to destruction'. Along with sorrow there must surely be pride at how the people of Britain faced up to it. During the First World War Centenary, we remember not just the leaders and the millions who served, but also the courage of small, disparate groups facing a powerful enemy: the signs of their effort – and often of their sacrifice – are there in your town. Also described are the main sites and how to get to them, which I hope will help you to set out on your personal quest to find this generation and to honour them.

The fifty-two months of war created a changed future as well as a threatening present, forcing an acceleration of personal, social and economic change with results for years to come. Here we trace the presence of the war in the British Isles – the key sites where this change took place.

The changes followed from the extraordinary effort of popular mobilisation. The cost in lives and disability was enormous. Familiar now – but not then – are the pictures of large cemeteries, but there is another side to the story: pride in success. The War Memorial outside St George's Hall in Liverpool recorded 'Out of the North Country came a mighty host ...' This generation met the challenge of a front line 60 miles from the Kent Coast (reduced to 40 miles by the German offensive in April 1918). From 1916 onwards gunfire could often be heard inland. This generation experienced the first air attacks, where Zeppelins roamed for hours over much of England. In the war at sea there were changes in the axis of threat, with a shift from mines and cruisers in the North Sea to submarines in the Atlantic approaches.

Many books were published recording the town and city experience. One of the best was *Leeds in the Great War*:

> What was it like to be alive then? Let us see with your eyes and feel with your heart and brain the bursting of the news on a generation that hardly believed in the possibility of war, the continuous departure of the troops until all the young manhood of Leeds had gone, the return of the wounded, the arrival of the lists of those who would never return, the darkened streets, the shortened food supply, the searchlights sweeping the clouds at night, the alarm of a Zeppelin attack, the hope and the despair, and all the pathos and the riot, all the spontaneous outburst of feelings that defy analysis, when the Armistice came, and at last there was an end.[1]

The book went on to pay tribute to the 'unparalleled endurance of pain and suffering shown by both sides and all classes and the wonderful power of organisation and initiative to meet unforeseen difficulties shown by our own country'.

On 27 October 1917, Prime Minister David Lloyd George (the first 'ranker' to reach the office) moved a vote of thanks in the House of Commons to the officers, non-commissioned officers and men of the British armies in the field. 'Our expeditionary force numbered at the

The spirit of service: relatives of Paul Stamper (English Heritage lead on the First World War) in Leicestershire, names unknown.

beginning of the war 160,000 men. Our expeditionary force today numbers over 3,000,000, probably the greatest feat of military organisation in the history of the world.'[2]

One year later, on 29 October 1918, the British Army was able to mount a victory parade through Lille, where fit and well-equipped troops marched through the city for two and a half hours to the delirious joy of the local citizens after four long years of harsh occupation, cut off from all contact with their partners or families in France and living under threat of starvation, execution and deportation.[3] A few days later there were similar scenes in Belgian towns that had been occupied by the German Army.

This was a war of small crews and sections: pilots in single-seater aircraft and workers by the machine in the munitions factory; the trawler crew sweeping mines in rough winter seas; the infantry section in a shell hole on the Western Front; the woman workers in the eleventh hour of a shift filling shells; the Royal Flying Corps pilot freezing at 8,000ft without oxygen. The war depended on their courage and initiative. Battle destroyed hierarchy. The command-and-control gap once battle had started has been well recognised for the Western Front, where troops might be cut off for hours, but there was a similar gap in many other situations in an age before instant communication. Members of small teams were on their own, with the higher command hours away. This was as true at sea and in the air as on the Western Front.

The war led to seven key changes:

1. A new industrial world managed by 'men of push and go'. Between the 'lions' and the 'donkeys' came the managers. By 1916:

> The whole of the North Country and the whole of the Midlands have in fact become a vast arsenal. Standing on an eminence in the North, one may by day watch ascending the smoke of from 400 to 500 munitions works, and by night at many a point in the Midland counties one may survey an encircling zone of flames as they belch forth from the chimneys of the engineering works of war.[4]

British industry had to take to mass production and giant factories of a kind rarely seen before the war. The largest was Gretna Green, some 9 miles long:

> One remembers coming past Gretna for the last time during the war in the gathering gloom of an autumn evening and strangely impressive it was in the half light. The place set on a turf bog with nitric and sulphuric acid plant and great leaden basins in which the dangerous materials were handled had a sinister aloof air well suited to its grim business.[5]

Munitions works were sited in open country with low hills behind them (Chilwell, Banbury and Gretna), in order to contain explosions. The Arsenal at Woolwich extended to 700 acres and at its peak in 1918 employed some 70,000 people. For the first time the UK came to know mass production and the American innovation of assembly lines. Most of the pre-war production had come from workshops and mills; the First World War demanded the introduction of the modern factory, with the government paying for extensions at every pre-war industrial site. Every valley wore a rim of fire.

2. Millions were on the move, the new soldiers to camps and civilians to the cities. London, Birmingham and Glasgow expanded. The main newcomers to the big cities were women and young adults. In Birmingham, in the 1911 census, males over 18 numbered 246,881 and females 283,366. By the spring of 1918 the respective totals were 200,251 and 323,911.[6]

The Munitions Works – a rim of fire in every valley.

Millions were on the move. This 1915 postcard is from Auntie Eliza living in Pocklington, Yorkshire, to her nephew Jack.

Much of the coast became a restricted area from Southampton round to Hull, with training grounds, airfields (142 landing strips in Kent alone) and naval bases in the Dover Straits and Harwich. There were seaplane and dirigible bases at Yarmouth and Folkestone and further north the repair base at Invergordon and the main base of the Grand Fleet at Scapa Flow. Smaller towns like Todmorden and Hove lost residents, as the men went into the army and the women to the munitions works. The countryside also changed, with 2 million more acres under the plough and the first use of 4,000 American Ford tractors (government-owned). The word 'allotment' was more widely used and thousands dug plots, some on railway embankments. By 31 December 1917 there were 185,147 allotments reported.[7]

3. New groups with political and economic influence. According to suffragist and early feminist Dame Millicent Fawcett, women began the war as serfs and ended it as independent citizens. Women at the Wimbledon train depot in early 1915 were the first to wear trousers – inspiration for the later trouser suit.[8] (Munitions workers in France and Germany continued to wear long skirts.) The role of women was vital, not just in munitions but in the transport system and in farming. The expansion of UK farming output in 1917 was one more vital contribution, but women were not the only group of new contributors. The war saw the coming of more affluent teenagers as young workers in the six years before conscription. They also served as boy scouts on guard duty and as messengers. For many there was access to training and expertise. The main losers were older men, excluded from Poor Law accommodation converted into hospitals. Rising prices ate into the unchanged 5s pension.

4. Changes in class relations. The lady and her maid could both be employed in the same munitions works. Lloyd George recorded in his memoirs for 1915 Balfour's experience when, invited as a venerable ex-prime minister to sit in on negotiations about dilution (the effect of female entry into the workforce in terms of pay and conditions) in a room off Whitehall containing Queen Anne's throne, 'He saw those stalwart artisans leaning against and sitting on the steps of the throne of the dead Queen and on equal terms negotiating conditions with the government of the day upon a question vitally affecting the conduct of a great war. Queen Anne was indeed dead.'[9] (Though it should be remembered that despite 1 million women being members of trade unions in 1918, by the beginning of the 1930s a woman's wage had returned to the pre-war rate of half that of her male co-worker in *more* industries than previously.) King George V, as part of the munitions drive, inaugurated the first meet-the-people tours. He praised the munitions work: 'Words like these uttered "man to man" ran like wildfire through the works.'[10]

New currents of social mobility affected the army, as General Douglas Haig recorded in his final despatch:

> A schoolmaster, a lawyer, a taxicab driver and an ex-sergeant major have commanded brigades: a mess sergeant, a railway signalman, a coal miner, a market gardener, an assistant secretary to a haberdashers company, a quartermaster sergeant and many private soldiers have risen to command battalions; clerks have commanded batteries.[11]

In the German Army there were some very strong pleas for promotion on merit so as to place the most efficient officers in positions of higher command: 'The military cabinet in Berlin was not to be moved by such propositions.'[12] Division remained in opportunities and accents but the working class was no longer a discrete social body and some considered that social changes 'created a sense of unease in the population'.[13]

5. Rising living standards. For many, especially in the new munitions factories, the war brought better pay and much improved living standards. Civilian mortality and infant mortality dropped sharply. There is a remarkable photograph (*see* p. 14) of young boys of the same school year in Bermondsey in 1894 and 1924 and most of the obvious change took place under wartime conditions. There were fears of food shortages and queues in 1917 but the Rhondda scheme of rationing shared out the available supplies according to the new ration book (*see* p. 188). There was a reduction in alcohol consumption: beer production fell from 36 million barrels in 1914 to 14 million in 1917 (and the beer was weaker)[14] and spirits production for domestic consumption was banned. The higher earnings were spent on food not drink, and not just in Carlisle and Enfield, where the pubs were nationalised. With rising living standards came mass entertainment and cinema-going. Charlie Chaplin became the first star (though much of the additional earnings of his fans went to buy war bonds).

6. Reshaping the transport system. The railways were used more intensively and came to be the main carriers of heavy freight, as coastal shipping was blocked by the submarine threat. The railway companies had to find routes across the Thames to the south coast. They also adapted to local commuting to large munitions plants on isolated sites, which had to draw their workforce from a wide area.

Progress across the war: boys of the same age in a school in Bermondsey, London in
1894 and 1924.

This was the beginning of the motor age, replacing the horse with the truck and the car. By 1920 the horse was relegated to local traffic. The war also saw the coming of the working-class driver as well as the woman driver.

7. The rise in power of the state over every aspect of the citizen's lives. This started with the 8 million letters sent to every household as a joint message from all political parties in 1914. Soon after, the Defence of the Realm Act (DORA) gave government far-reaching discretionary powers. One key date was 15 August 1915. Under the National Registration Act, an army of 150,000 volunteers worked so that 'every male and female in Great Britain between the ages of fifteen and sixty-five was thereby registered on a separate card giving all the information necessary for recruiting and industrial purposes'.[15] In Birmingham the new Hollerith automatic equipment processed the cards. There was censorship, then conscription from 1917. State control extended even to the distribution of contraceptives. National efficiency became a matter for the new ministries in Whitehall. 'The most important of these were the Ministry of Shipping, the Ministry of Labour, the Ministry of Food and the Ministry of Pensions to which were added at later dates the Ministry of Reconstruction, the Ministry of National Service and the Ministry of the Air.'[16]

> The war and all it connoted filled people's minds. Everything one did or read or thought was coloured by it. The war's effects at home and abroad, its bearing on the relationships of life and national affairs, its searching of the heart and stirring of the conscience, kept people at high tension.
>
> Such relief as Leeds people were able to obtain from the common strain, the almost monotonous round of war work and of ordinary duties done in unaccustomed circumstances, was afforded only by fleeting hours of relaxation at theatres, cinemas and concerts or week-ends at holiday resorts. But even then one could not get away from reminders of the world crisis, from troubled thought and conversation concerning the next thing to be done; it all weighed heavily as the burden borne by Bunyan's pilgrim when he set forth with the cry 'What shall I do to be saved?'[17]

The war was thought to have changed everything:

> There are many persons who firmly believe that the intense gunfire often induced rain and caused cold winds. In south-east England

No. of Certificate   M921447

Army Form D 455

SEPARATION ALLOWANCE and ALLOTMENT OF PAY.

Certificate of Identity for wife or child or other relative of a Soldier.

Notice:—This Certificate is Government Property. It is no security whatever for Debt. Any person improperly detaining it as a pledge or security for debt is liable to a fine of Twenty Pounds, or in the case of a second offence to imprisonment with hard labour for a term of Six Months.

THIS IS TO CERTIFY that Mrs. *J. Proven* being the *Wife*

of No. *596 Glasgow* Rank and Name *Proven A.*

Regiment or Corps. *R.E.*

is entitled, subject to the Regulations, to payment of allowance at the Post Office

at *G.P.O. Dunfermline*

This Certificate is issued by (Signature) _____

Regimental Paymaster.

Date *14.4.14*   Army Pay Office, *Chatham.*

THE PAYEE SHOULD CAREFULLY READ THE FOLLOWING INSTRUCTIONS:—

1. This Certificate is the authority for the issue to you of your weekly allowance.

2. Payment is due each **Monday**, and will be made on production of this Certificate at the Post Office selected for payment.

3. Should you be ill and unable to go to the Post Office, send someone you can trust to go to the Post Office with your Identity Certificate, to ask the Postmaster for the Postal Draft, so that you can sign the Draft and get the Sick Certificate on the back signed also. The Postmaster will hold the Certificate until the signed Draft is brought back to him. Then he will return it to the bringer with the money for you.

4. As payment cannot be made without this Certificate it should be taken great care of. If it is lost you should at once inform the issuing office and also the Postmaster.

5. Notice should be given to the Postmaster in any case where it is desired to change the Post Office at which payment is made.

6. No person is entitled to receive separation allowance through more than one office or to be in possession of more than one of these certificates at the same time. If a second form is received it should be returned at once to the issuing office.

7. When writing about these allowances always quote the number of this certificate and state the soldier's regimental number, full name, regiment, and the Post Office at which payment is made. Any change of address should be at once notified to the issuing office.

8. Any circumstance affecting the rate of the allowance, such as the birth or death of a child, should be reported at once to the issuing office.

9. This certificate must be returned to the issuing office directly the spaces for the Post Office stamp have all been filled up or directly the allowance ceases to be payable.

10. **If the Soldier is discharged this Certificate must be returned at once to the Regimental Paymaster, as no further payment of Separation Allowance or Allotment is due. Any attempt to procure payment after the soldier's discharge may be made the subject of legal proceedings.**

D. D. & L., London, E.C
(Pcops) Wt. W8305/M903 500,000 16/16 W 27

Forms
D. 455
14

Post Office Date Stamp.

N.B.—Postmasters are warned not to make any payment after the last ring space on this certificate has been stamped.

[CONTINUED OVERLEAF.

The New State; Separation Allowance for Mrs J. Proven Dunfermline for Private A.E. Proven serving Royal Engineers Chatham.

the wetness was phenomenal during the war and it is certainly remarkable that the meteorological conditions prevailing in Great Britain should have been so abnormal.[18]

The History of Leeds and other sources presented the main phases of the war at home year by year, which we can summarise as follows:

1914: Shock of war – the inconceivable became real. Build-up of military training. Kitchener and the New Army. Disasters at sea and bombardment of Scarborough and other coastal towns.

1915: Intensive training. Zeppelin raids frequent. Building of new war economy. Sinking of *Lusitania*.

1916: New war economy in full swing. Somme casualties in every home. Coasts and air quieter.

1917: Rigid system of fuel and food control, leading to ration books for all. Gotha Raids and intensive war against U-boats.

1918: Grim determination to carry on. King's call for Intercession on first Sunday of 1918. Great shock of German March Offensive. Fast-moving political and military events. The war then finished as suddenly and unexpectedly as it had started at the eleventh hour of the eleventh day of the eleventh month.

The Zeppelin raid on the night of 31 March to 1 April 1916, when Zeppelins were roaming over the UK.

The beginning of the end: Zeppelin L15 sinking off the Kentish Coast on 1 April 1916, brought down by anti-aircraft fire.

The wider Western Front stretched back from the battle zones into most of the UK and beyond into the worldwide supply operation. Where were the key sites for this national mobilisation? How did this generation meet a challenge greater than that faced by any other since the English Civil War, 270 years earlier?

Notes

1 Scott, W.H., *Leeds in the Great War*, Leeds City Council, 1923, p. xi.
2 Lloyd George, *Hansard*, 27 October 1917.
3 McPhail, Helen, *The Long Silence*, Taurus, 1999, p. 193.
4 Yates, L.K., *The Woman's Part: A Record of Munition Work*, Hodder and Stoughton, p. 8.
5 Dewar, G.A.B., *The Great Munitions Feat*, Constable, 1921, p. 133.
6 Brazier, R.H. and Sandford. E., *Birmingham in the Great War*, Cornish Brothers, 1921, p. 286.
7 *The War Cabinet, Report for the Year 1917*, Cd 9005, HMSO, 1918.
8 Pratt, E.A., *British Railways in the Great War*, Selwyn and Blount, 1919, p. 456.
9 Lloyd George, David, *War Memoirs of David Lloyd George*, Ivor Nicholson and Watson, Vol. II, 1933, p. 296.
10 Lloyd George, David, *War Memoirs*, p. 321.
11 Boraston, J.H. (ed.), *Sir Douglas Haig's Despatches*, Dent, 1979, p. 348.
12 Vagts, A., *History of Militarism*, Meridian, 1959, p. 234.
13 Cooksley, P., *The Home Front: Civilian Life in World War One*, Tempus, 2006, p. 116.
14 *War Cabinet Report 1917*, London, 1918, p. xiii.
15 Williams, B., *Raising and Training the New Armies*, Constable, 1918, p. 22.
16 *War Cabinet Report 1917*, p. vii.
17 *Leeds in the Great War*, p. 38.
18 Gladstone, W., *Birds in the Great War*, p. 71.

1

The British Army

I called upon the energy of the country to supply deficiencies in previous experience and preparation, and set to work to build a series of new armies, complete in all their branches (Kitchener, June 1916).[1]

The original British Expeditionary Force (BEF) fought in the Retreat from Mons in 1914 and then at Ypres. Next came the New Army – Kitchener's Army – and the 141 days of the Somme battle. Last came the conscript army of 1918 with vastly increased firepower – from fifteen rounds of rifle fire a minute (and no grenades) to a million shells a day.

The Army had shifted deployment in the ten years before the war from the empire to a possible war across the Channel. The effective reforms under War Secretary Edward Cardwell in 1870 had created a linked battalion system so that within each regiment one battalion served at home and one overseas. In practice the understrength home battalion was creating drafts for the priority battalion overseas and the fifteen-year postings of the Cardwell overseas battalions weakened the ties with their home area. Even as late as 1938 the 2nd Battalion Royal Welch Fusiliers (the regiment of Siegfried Sassoon and Robert Graves and in which my father served) was sent to Lucknow for a posting that was expected to last to 1953.

R.B. Haldane, the reforming war minister after 1906, sought a 'Hegelian' army, named after the German philosopher Friedrich Hegel, seer of transformation, and transform he did. The British Army of 1910 was totally different from that of 1905. At its core was an expeditionary force of regulars, six divisions each of 12,000 men, which could be brought into line across the Channel in twenty days. For home defence against invasion there were the Territorials, potentially another fourteen divisions, but ones that required further training and armaments. There was one omission in the scheme – a stockpile of rifles, guns and ammunition to bring about this expansion. The scheme created an army with many more men but with quite inadequate armaments,

The War Office. A massive building and one of the first in London on concrete caissons.

mainly because extra money had to be found for building dreadnought battleships. The Haldane reorganisation had to fund a large expansion with a static budget.

With new organisation came some new men. Haldane brought in modernisers such as Haig, who were responsible for implementation. The one constant was the regimental system – in fact the new organisation strengthened the local roots by basing the bulk of the army at home. Recruitment was voluntary and the new system provided greater opportunities. The reservation of certain jobs – police and London taxi drivers – for ex-servicemen also helped improve prospects for those who had finished their seven-year enlistment.

The new War Office was opened in 1906, across Whitehall from the Horse Guards, the old headquarters.[2] The War Office was a massive trapezium resting on a concrete caisson base 6ft thick and 30ft below road level, in order to stop it from sinking into the Thames mud. The building had an ornately decorated hall with a grand staircase. Along the roof, sculpted figures symbolised peace and war, truth and justice, fame and victory, and on top of each of the four corner towers a decorative dome masked the irregularity of the building's shape. The lion in the coat of arms over the main entrance has a distinctive snarl.

The Lion Rampant of the War Office.

The reforms in the ten years before 1914 included:

A new General Staff: there were some efficient heads of branches, even though the central leadership remained woefully inadequate until Field Marshal Sir William Robertson took over as Chief of the Imperial General Staff (CIGS) in 1915.
A new, clearly written operational guide: 'Field Service Regulations' in two volumes.
A balloon corps and then from 1912 the Royal Flying Corps: both within the army. The Royal Air Force followed from 1 April 1918.
The use of heavy tractors for pulling artillery.
The use of telephones to transmit orders.
New emphasis on intensive training symbolised by training for fifteen aimed rounds a minute at Hythe Ranges. Soldiers had to pass this test or leave the army.
Large-scale divisional exercises on Salisbury Plain (newly leased for training) with air observation.
The reorganisation of the RAMC (Royal Army Medical Corps) to focus on prevention and sanitary measures as well as on treatment, following the success of the Japanese medical services in the Russo-Japanese War of 1904–05.

Military activity permeated society. The new Territorials were recruited in the towns, while the old Yeomanry cavalry had been based in the counties controlled by the Lords Lieutenants. The Boy Scouts, with their handsome uniforms, were founded by Boer War hero Baden Powell. The young Clement Attlee drilled the boys in the Haileybury Boys Club and gained early promotion in 1914 as a result.[3] By 1914 half a million people were taking part in military activity, 300,000 in the Territorial Army.

From August 1914 Kitchener and the War Office drove through more changes, first with the New Army. Kitchener called for the first 100,000 volunteers. He was one of the few to see the need for an army of 2 million men, which would have to serve abroad in a long war. The Territorials were only pledged to serve at home and it is not clear whether they could have been expanded at the rate required.

Kitchener's call to arms was more than the one poster – it was a sustained and powerful publicity campaign carried out by the relatively new method of street posters on hoardings. This media campaign used shame (what will your girl think of you?) as well as appeals to patriotism. Over the next two years there were 2 million volunteers.[4] The new army was, however, trained by old officers. The 'dugouts' who had been retired by the modernisers returned for a time.

Lord Roberts' Christmas card 1913. There was a move towards greater military activity across society.

Lord Kitchener at the War Office, in his first days as War Minister, with 'Bob's your
uncle' Lord Roberts. From *The Kitchener Memorial Book*.

THE COUNTRY CALL
911 THE THE
310.000 MEN
GO NOW

WANTED AT ONCE
5000
RECRUITS FROM LEEDS
BRITISH BULLDOGS
AIREDALE or YORKSHIRE TERRIER

NAW THEN JOHN WILLIE
- GER AGATE LAD -
. JOIN T'ARMY .

BERLIN

GOD SAVE THE KING

E LEEDS "PALS" 2ⁿᵈ BATTALION RECRUITING CAR. Sep 19

The Leeds Pals recruiting car – 'Naw then, John Willis – ger agate lad join t'army' –
on to Berlin.

There were great regional and local differences in recruitment rates.
It was more of a tartan army than it statistically should have been; the
recruitment rate was much higher in Scotland, and higher in urban
than in rural areas.[5]

Recruitment up to 4 November 1914 per 10,000 population:

Southern Scotland, 237
Midlands, 196
Lancashire, 178
London and the Home Counties, 170
Yorkshire and the North East, 150
Ireland (North and South), 127
West of England, 88
Eastern England, 80

By early 1915 most of the original BEF were casualties and Territorial
divisions (inadequately equipped and trained) were drafted in. These
just managed to hold the 20-mile front around Ypres up to May 1915,

John gets to camp: advance party of the Leeds Pals unloading Quaker Oats at Colsterdale.

Sketches of Tommy's life At the Base. — N° 3

When I got ready to go to bed, I found I was kindly permitted to sleep on a triangular space large enough to accomodate a small slice of mince pie

A postcard depicting life in camp.

when German attention turned East. The British line was held mainly
as result of the Flanders mud, detested but in fact the secret defensive
weapon both in containing any advance and limiting the effectiveness
of what was, at this point, massive German superiority in artillery.
A contemporary, J.F.C. Fuller (later to be one of the best known military writers of the twentieth century), wrote:

> These months (the winter of 1914–15) were some of the wettest on
> record: The British line was waist deep in mud. Yet it was the mud
> of Flanders which saved this thin line from annihilation in spite of its
> swearing. Had Flanders been a dry, open plain instead of a swamp, it
> is not too much to suppose that the war would have been over by the
> summer of 1915.[6]

This period saw a great shortage of young officers after the very heavy
casualties among battalion commanders in the First Battle of Ypres in
1914, and then among junior officers in the 1915 offensives at Neuve
Chapelle and Loos. It was an army with a desperate mission but a
shortage of experienced leaders. Later Haig wrote that it had been a
near-miracle that the line held in 1915. It was the year that saw the
greatest disparity in weaponry and training between the British and
German armies.

In 1916 the New Army mounted its 141 days of offensive on the
Somme. Then came a new wave of recruits – the conscripts – either
older men who had not volunteered or 18-year-olds. The old distinc-
tions between the Territorials and Kitchener's men were blurred. The
conscripts were the first in British history.[7]

By 1918 the army had completely changed again. This required
a massive logistic operation with each mile of front requiring 2,000
tons of supplies per day. It had support in canteens, repair bases, road-
mending and many other activities. It was machine war with new sections that had not existed in 1914, such as the Tank Corps, the Machine
Gun Corps (170,000 at its peak) and Royal Flying Corps (Royal Air
Force from 1 April 1918). Notable too was the Special Brigade, for
discharging poison gas via the feared and effective Livens projectors.
There was also a whole range of new and improved weapons including
Stokes mortars, Lewis guns, the lighter Vickers-Maxim machine gun,
tanks and sound-ranging artillery (aided by accurate maps and aerial
observation). The 100 days of advance from June to November 1918
was a faster-moving mechanised war, even if slowed by the German
use of mustard gas, which was only available to the British from September 1918.

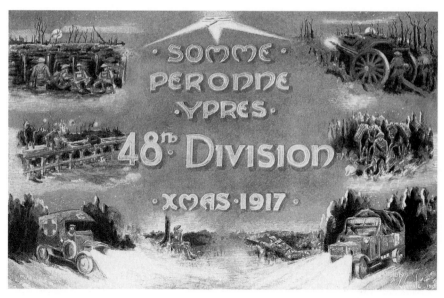

A 1917 48th division Christmas card from Fred, wishing you all 'a happy Christmas and prosperous New Year'. What happened to Fred?

This was not the old trench warfare in fixed lines. Even in static positions trenches were moved to avoid aerial observation. If the war had continued as expected in 1919 it would have gone underground, as demonstrated by a recently excavated network of deep caverns 40ft below the surface around Ypres. By mid-1918 only 450,000 out of the 1.4 million British troops on the Western Front were front-line infantry. Divisions were reduced from twelve to nine battalions of infantry. The line lengthened – the British Army was, by early 1918, holding 122 miles with this limited number of front-line infantry. The massive artillery and machine-gun presence came to be the primary defence, as it was later for attack.

The new machine war needed much more maintenance and the mechanics needed much more supply. There was even a special workshop to produce rubber stamps – 57,107 of them in 1918.[8] All the improved weaponry needed more training, leading to specialist training courses being vastly expanded. Risks, of course, were not equally shared, with heavy casualties among infantry, while 2,592 of the Army Service Corps (314,693 by 1918) were killed in action during the whole war – possibly fewer than would have died in the air pollution and performing the heavy labour of town life in the UK.[9] There was also a huge salvage operation of people via rehabilitation of the wounded, and also of materials such as metal and leather. Such salvage of metals was a vital step towards reducing calls on shipping.

Middlesbrough War Memorial has one of the longest lists of names in the UK. (This photograph shows only one half of the memorial.)

These changes created new winners and losers. Young conscripts and those with little education were drafted to the infantry. Those with more education or technical expertise were sent to the expanding number of support services. On 1 September 1914 infantry was 53.9 per cent of the strength in France. By 1 November 1918 it was 31.3 per cent.[10] The first volume of the Official History for 1914 paid tribute to the British soldier:

> The British Army gained much useful experience on the Aisne, and absolute confidence in its shooting. The men learned how to entrench quickly and how to appreciate the value of digging. The drafts were able to settle down, and the young soldiers of the Special Reserve had time to gather instruction from the trained officers and N.C.O.s who, though sadly reduced in numbers, were still fairly abundant. For the rest, the soldiers astonished even those who trained them by their staunchness, their patience, their indomitable cheerfulness under incessant hardship, and, in spite of a fire which no human being had ever before experienced, by their calm, cool courage at all times. Whether it was the gunner unloading ammunition almost too hot to handle, in the midst of blazing wagons; the engineer repairing his bridge under continuous fire; the infantryman patiently enduring heavy shellfire, patrolling no-man's-land in the hours of darkness, or, as a sniper, lying all night on soaking clay in dripping beet fields; the

transport driver guiding his wagons through bursting shells; or the stretcher bearer toiling though the dark hours to rescue the wounded; all alike proved themselves worthy soldiers of the King. Though their dearest friends, comrades of many years, fell beside them, they fought with the majesty of their ancestors, without anger or malice, trusting always in the good cause of their country. Their good health in quagmires of trenches under constant rain of itself testified to their discipline. Sober, temperate and self-respecting, they were not to be discouraged by wounds or sickness. There could be no fear as to the final victory, if only armies of such soldiers could be brought into being in sufficient numbers without delay and, conveyed in security across the Channel to France.[11]

Aldershot, Hampshire

This was the base both for the BEF and for Kitchener's Army and remains the home of the British Army. Aldershot was a purpose-built military town, a site chosen by Prince Albert after the Crimean War, and developed as a service town as well as a military town. There were many support services, including the largest military printer and publisher in Gale and Polden, tailoring, provisions and hostelries led by the Queen's Hotel, and a golf course. Training grounds were more sheltered than on Salisbury Plain and not so far away from the barracks. There were large houses for the commanders, including the largest for the commandant, and a library donated by Prince Albert (which is still in use); furthermore, it was within easy reach of London. In this army home all ranks passed each other on the roads and there was much competitive sport.

There was, and still is, a wide central road on Queen's Avenue with parade grounds on one side and barracks on the other. Most of the First World War generals had served there, including Haig, French and Robertson, who, in his memoirs, wrote of his later service and promotion:

Once more [...] fortune had favoured me and the advancement was more gratifying because it had occurred at Aldershot where on a miserable November night thirty years before, I had entered the cavalry barracks as a recruit – a lonely and for all practical purposes a seemingly friendless lad.[12]

For his portrait in the book, Robertson chose a photograph not by a studio photographer, like most, but a snapshot by an American

Queens Avenue in Aldershot – the front entrance to the home of the British Army.

The Smith-Dorrien Welfare Centre in Aldershot. General Smith-Dorrien was popular at Aldershot but was later sacked at Ypres by Robertson, supposedly with the words ''Orace you're for home'.

soldier in a parade at Coblenz after the war. Aldershot was also the home of the RAMC with a new headquarters and training base built before 1914.

The Commander's House is still there, together with many of the original barrack buildings. There is faint lettering on the front of the Smith-Dorrien Welfare Centre, organised by the later commander at Le Cateau and Ypres. It is now being refurbished. The layout and some of the special atmosphere is still there, in part preserved in the excellent museum. There has been considerable new development in recent years and Aldershot is no longer fated to decline into a military ghost town. Much of the BEF in 1914 left from Aldershot and the railway sidings from which they went to Southampton are still to be seen on North Lane.

Hythe, Kent

The School of Musketry was founded in 1853 on the sand dunes near Folkestone for training in the use of the new Enfield (later Lee Enfield) rifle. This rifle was modified so that it had a shorter barrel and could fire clips rather than single shots. It was reliable and easily cleaned. It was at Hythe in 1909 that the School Director, Colonel McMahon, decided to improve marksmanship to fifteen aimed rounds a minute in order to make up for the deficiency in machine guns: 'We must train every soldier in our army to become a human machine gun.'[13] This was double the rate of fire of other armies. McMahon aimed to:

> … look to our past military history and fall back on traditions now six centuries old. We must aim at producing the same superiority of fire with our rifles as we had obtained with the long-bow in the 14th century.

This gave the retreating BEF in 1914 an advantage in firepower, as the ample supply of German machine guns, weighing in at 220lb each, proved to be too heavy for an advance that involved marching 125 miles in ten days. During the retreat from Mons the British rifle fire was mistaken for machine-gun fire. According to a German official source: 'The enemy's superiority in machine-guns (and other weapons) was two-fold, three-fold, even four-fold.' As the German Army commander von Kluck later wrote: 'I always had the greatest admiration for the BEF, it was the wonderful kernel of a great army. The way the retreat was carried out was remarkable.' The ranges are still outside the town of Hythe and are still in use, but can be glimpsed from the road going towards Dymchurch and Dungeness.

Knowsley, Lancashire

It was here in the grounds of Knowsley House, near Liverpool, that the first Pals Battalion, raised from local groups, was trained – the nucleus of the Kitchener armies. The Pals Battalion was first proposed by Lord Derby at a meeting in St George's Hall, Liverpool, on the evening of 28 August 1914, and the first battalion was trained in the grounds of his estate at Knowsley. In the months after, nearly every town raised one or more Kitchener battalion. It was to be a whole army of Pals Battalions, many recruited from middle-class occupations, thus avoiding the stigma which hung over recruits to the old army. The Pals were trained at local bases and could live at home; it would have been impossible to find barracks or training grounds on a centralised basis for one million recruits. 'Recruitment and training was by local initiative rather than by elderly, fussy and incompetent generals in Whitehall.'[14]

Kitchener supplied a flair for communication, with such phrases as 'the First Hundred Thousand' and 'the Last Million'. Referring to his pre-war conviction that the conflict would be a long one, he stated (in his last speech in the House of Lords, three days before his death): 'I relied upon the energy of the country to supply deficiencies in previous experience and preparations.'

Salisbury Plain, Wiltshire

The base here was expanded partly to make up for the limited size of the training grounds at Aldershot and Woolwich. From the A303, the main road west, the plain stands out as a massive and sinister shape on the horizon. Originally the plan was to provide tents without permanent accommodation, but already in 1902–3, brick barracks were built at Tidworth in the north-east of the plain. A railway spur was built from Amesbury to Bulford Camp. During the war there was a vast expansion in tents and in wooden huts: 'Tented camps sprang up all over the plain.' Development was particularly extensive around Larkhill.[15]

The plain developed a bad reputation for discomfort and lack of amenities even after huts replaced tents. The first visitors, the

A view across the Salisbury Plain from the chalk New Zealand Kiwi at Bulford.

Building huts at Larkhill on Salisbury Plain; those who were sent there were in no position to complain.

Canadians, had an epidemic of cerebro-spinal meningitis and although this was not repeated, the other problems remained. The nearest town of any size was 20 miles away; the plain was a vast expanse of heath swept by wind and rain, possibly more desolate than when the builders of Stonehenge worked. Between Stonehenge and the British Army, there had been little settlement there. The plain is a plateau, highly exposed, and, even now, the largest wild grassland in north-west Europe. It was not a place for generals, who tended to stay in Aldershot, but for basic training, for both infantry and artillery. Those who were sent there were in no position to complain and (probably) those who were in a position to do so did not go there.

The plain was shared between infantry and artillery, with the artillery mainly based at Larkhill. The artillery ranges had moved there from Woolwich, after local citizens had complained about the damage to their houses from shells fired across Woolwich Common. It was not until after the First World War that Larkhill became the exclusive preserve of the artillery. During the war it was shared with the infantry and (until 1916) also with the Royal Flying Corps. The first army flying base was at Larkhill. The aircraft hangars or sheds are still there, together with a section of the tarmac from the runway. This ran south to north, and at the end was a 70ft drop down a steep hillside to help the low-powered craft get airborne. The Royal Flying Corps had to move, however, as the artillery range expanded. The new Central Flying School was set on the northern edge of the plain at Upavon.

Salisbury Plain was also the main base for Dominion armies, with New Zealanders at Bulford (leaving a kiwi carved on the hillside) and Australians (after 1915) at Codford and Sutton Veny on the west of the plain, with their rising-sun insignia still carved on the downs.[16] This was a pleasanter billet in the more sheltered valley of the River Wylye, although even further from any town. It also had some shops and pubs.

Grantham, Lincolnshire

In 1915 the Machine Gun Corps – the largest new organisation for the British Army in the First World War – was set up. This followed on from the success of the machine-gun training organised in France by a serial military entrepreneur, Baker-Carr. Between the lions and the donkeys came the managers and Baker-Carr was a formidable specimen of the breed, well chronicled in his later autobiography *From Chauffeur to Brigadier*.[17] The Machine Gun Corps numbered 177,000 at its peak and most were trained near Grantham, where Lord Brownlow lent land near his ancestral seat of Belton Park. The training school was allowed to work there on condition that it was not visible from the house. This still left room for 400 huts, which were built on the slope going down to Grantham.

The Machine Gun School also inherited a Grantham innovation – the world's first uniformed policewomen, recruited in late 1914 for supervision of troops with a fearsome but to some extent undeserved reputation from Manchester and Liverpool, who were bound for Gallipoli. Grantham benefited from the huge influx of relatively well-paid machine-gunners. Among the busiest suppliers would have been Alfred Roberts, assistant manager of a local grocery shop and later father of Margaret Thatcher, née Roberts. Alfred was a determined man: he tried to join up no fewer than six times and was rejected on medical grounds on each occasion. The training at Grantham was later described by the 19-year-old Arthur Russell in *The Machine Gunner*:

The 51st Division Machine Gunners trained at Grantham, on 23 March 1918.

Our training was most intensive and strenuous. From 8.30 in the morning to mid day and from one o'clock to five the parade ground resounded to the sharp commands of our numerous instructors giving orders: Mount Gun; Fire; Fall Out; Dismount gun and such like commands. For hours at a stretch we would run for distances of twenty-five to fifty yards with the forty eight pound tripod, the thirty eight pound machine gun, and boxes containing belts of ammunition each weighing twenty one pounds.[18]

His morale was improved by recognition of the high quality of the Vickers-Maxim and later the Lewis gun. The Vickers-Maxim was water cooled, lighter than the German Maxim and more reliable than the air-cooled French Hotchkiss. For the Hotchkiss the barrel distorted after 500 rounds (a common feature of air-cooled weapons), while the Vickers-Maxim could fire 60,000 rounds in a day and retain accuracy. The Lewis gun was by far the best light machine gun that could be carried by one man. The Machine Gun Corps was disbanded after the war and there is no official history. Its memorial, with the inscription 'Saul has slain his thousands and David his ten thousands', caused a storm of controversy after the war. It stands at Hyde Park Corner in central London, near the memorial for another arm that gained more sinister reputation than public thanks – the Second World War's Bomber Command.

Sandhurst, Berkshire

This had been the centre for officer training in the British Army since 1821. Any new officers were trained after selection from the ranks in a shortened but effective six-month course. The maintenance of standards in officer training and selection was vital to the improved war effort, and a key standard was that officers should be responsible for the well-being of their men. The expectation was quite different in the German and French armies, where officers were remote figures and daily supervision was left to sergeants.

Royal Engineers, Chatham, Kent

The Royal Engineers' contribution was vital in providing a whole range of support services on the Western Front, including roads, water supply and the construction of Nissen and other huts in the

The Raid
" Bert! It's our officer !"

Cartoonist Bruce Bairnsfather on officers –
such bonds not always in the British Army
but unthinkable in any other First World
War army.

rear areas. Behind the German lines there were towns and villages
that could provide shelter. The areas behind the British lines were
sparsely populated and most housing had been damaged by shellfire.
The army came to rely on the invention of the Canadian/American
Major Nissen of 29th Company Royal Engineers – a hut made of corrugated iron that was waterproof and fireproof.[19] Although this was
the most familiar hut, with some 100,000 constructed, there were
other types including the portable Tarrant hut, made of wood, and
the portable Liddell hut, which could be made either of wood or of
corrugated iron. The Nissen hut was extraordinarily important for
army welfare. One memoir of the Somme expresses gratitude for this
simple construction:

> Mid November saw us exchanging billets for the line in another of
> those relays (periods outside the line) which enabled the British Army
> to survive the duty of garrisoning in the appalling winter of 1916–
> 17. We spent several days in the fatigue camp at Fricourt where we
> scraped mud off the roads all day long. Then we moved on a stage
> to Montauban. Here a wonderful change has taken place. Rows of
> Nissen Huts had sprung into being with raised duckboard tracks
> well above ground level and wide corduroy track ran from the main
> Albert Road to the huts containing the Quartermaster's Stores.[20]

The army also relied on the engineers for water and sanitation; providing water for 2 million men in areas without springs involved digging many boreholes down to 1,000ft. Unlike the French Army, where lack of water at the front in Champagne created the bearded *poilu* or hairy one, the British Army had enough water to shave and, during reliefs, to take baths 'often with hot water' in brewery vats. Another never-ending task was the construction and servicing of incinerators. All these skills and more were taught by the Royal Engineers from their base in Chatham. They also moved under the front line, tunnelling and mining, a warfront upon which the British Army developed a marked advantage, culminating in the mining of the Messines Ridge in June 1917.

Shirehampton, Bristol; Ormskirk, Lancashire; Swaythling, Hampshire; Park Royal, London

These were the main centres for collection of horses and mules for the Western Front. The molly mule (and the male), among the thousands of animals who served with the British Army, was the forgotten heroine (and hero) of the Western Front – outshone by the glories of *Warhorse*. Although sometimes evil tempered she/he did more work and ate less than the horses. She was also less likely to be sick. The official history of the Veterinary Services reported that:

> Mortality among mules consequent upon transportation by land and sea was less than one-half that among horses.
>
> Mortality from disease and all causes in the field was less than one-half that among horses.
>
> Liability to disease, including mange, necessitating evacuation to veterinary hospitals was less than one-half that among horses.
>
> The mule could be kept in good condition on a food ration which was 25 per cent less than that of the average of the horse.[21]

Notably prized were American mules, bred outdoors on the Great Plains, which could stand in lines in winter, which, on the Western Front, were usually open. There was usually shelter for the men but much more rarely could this be managed for the animals. Over 200,000 American and Canadian mules were imported during the war. They arrived at Avonmouth, near Bristol; Latham Park, near Ormskirk; Liverpool; or Romsey, near Southampton. Park Royal had been opened up shortly before the war as a site for the Royal (Agricultural)

A mule team. Mules were the unsung heroes of the war and were widely used by the British Army.

Show and it was now pressed into service as a site for veterinary checks and training.

Perhaps deep in the night we can hear the ghostly braying of those thousands of animals who passed through Shirehampton and other bases. At least there is now a fine memorial to Animals in War at Park Lane, near Marble Arch. At this memorial the mule is in the lead – a starring role at last. During the war there had been some moving tributes. Colonel George Marshall (later the US Chief of Staff) recorded in April 1918, in Picardy:

> I found one day an elaborately decorated grave in a wood where the supply echelon of an infantry regiment was located. Over the grave was a large wooden cross with the following inscription:

> Here lies poor Nellie of the Supply
> Company of the Sixteenth Infantry
> Served in Texas, Mexico and France
> Wounded and killed near Villers
> Tournelles. She done her bit
> Nellie was an army mule.[22]

The horse was of course recognised – notably with the moving memorial at Chipilly, on the Somme, of the artilleryman with his wounded horse.[23] Recognition also came from Haig:

> If in March 1918 the equine force of Germany had been on the same scale and as efficient as the British equine force, then Germany would unquestionably have succeeded in breaking through between the French and British armies and inflicting a defeat so great that recovery would have been impossible.[24]

Shoeburyness, Essex

This became the home of the Army Dog Training School. As the battlefields became more churned up by shellfire, it was realised that dogs could be used as messengers, saving the lives of runners. The most suitable dogs were found to be collies, lurchers and Airedales. Dogs such as poodles (and all dogs with curly tails) were not suitable: 'This method of carrying the tail seems to indicate a certain levity of character, quite at variance with the serious duties required.'[25] Dogs were trained in groups at Shoeburyness. When new dogs were being trained, the older ones 'generally elected to watch the proceedings perched on the top of their kennels, and loud choruses of derision were hurled at the raw recruits'. The British war dogs were one-way dogs, with the keeper remaining in the rear and the dog taken to the front line to run back to the keeper, in contrast to the two-way dogs of the German Army. The German Army made more use of dogs and their barking could often be heard from the British trenches. British use of dogs came late. Unlike in the German Army, they were not used to seek out the wounded in no-man's-land, but from 1917 onwards they became widely used. The key manager was Lieutenant Colonel E.H. Richardson, director of the School in Shoeburyness.

Notes
1 Simkins, P., *Kitchener's Army: The Raising of the New Armies 1914–16*, Pen and Sword, 2007, p. 40.
2 *MoD: The Old War Office*, MoD, 2001.
3 Harris, K., *Attlee*, Weidenfeld and Nicolson, 1962, p. 19.
4 Anon., *Kitchener*, Memorial Book, 1916.
5 Gregory, A., *The Last Great War*, Cambridge University Press, 2008, p. 81.
6 Fuller, J.F.C., *Memoirs of an Unconventional Soldier*, Ivor Nicholson and Watson, 1936.
7 Bet-El, I.R., *Conscripts: Lost Legions of the Great War*, Sutton, 1999.
8 War Office, *Statistics of the Military Effort of the British Empire During the Great War (SMEBE), 1914–20*, London Stamp Exchange, 1992, p. 202.

9 *SMEBE*, p. 181.
10 *SMEBE*, p. 66.
11 Edmonds, *Military Operations France and Belgium*, Vol. 1, p. 410.
12 Robertson, W., *From Private to Field Marshal*, Constable, 1921, p. 153.
13 Pridham, C.H.B., *Superiority of Fire*, Hutchinson, 1945, p. 56.
14 Germains, V.W., *The Kitchener Armies: The Story of a National Achievement*, Peter Davis, 1930.
15 James, N.D.G., *Gunners at Larkhill*, Gresham Books, 1983.
16 Wyeth, R., *The Men of St Mary's & the ANZAC War Graves: The Parish Church of St Mary, Codford, Wiltshire*.
17 Baker Carr, C.D., *From Chauffeur to Brigadier*, Ernest Benn, 1930.
18 Russell, A., *The Machine Gunner*, Roundwood Press, 1977.
19 Engineers, history miscellaneous works, p. 177, p. 10.
20 Child, J., *The Gallant Company*, Sydney, 1930.
21 Blenkinsop, L.J. and Rainey, J.W., *Official History of the War Veterinary Services*, HMSO, 1925, p. 63.
22 Marshall, G.C., *My Service in the Great War*, Houghton Mifflin, 1976, p. 51.
23 Coombs, R., *Before Endeavours Fade*, Picador/After the Battle, 1976, p. 120.
24 Clabby, J., *The History of the Royal Army Veterinary Corps 1919–1961*, J.A. Allen, 1963, p. 18.
25 Richardson, E.H., *British War Dogs*, Skeffington and Son, n.d., p. 71.

2

The Allies – Shock Troops of the British Empire
– and the Associated Americans[1]

The Canadian contingent was an early arrival on the Western Front. The new Canadian Army was there from February 1915, a year before most of the new British Army. It had an outstanding record, firstly in courage in dealing with the first gas attack at Ypres in April 1915, and secondly for the capture of Vimy Ridge in April 1917. It took the lead in redesign of services for greater firepower and it served as a role model for the Australians.

General Monash, the Australian commander, later recorded: 'It is impossible to overvalue the advantages which accrued to the Canadian troops for their close, constant association of all the four divisions with each other, with the corps commander, his staff and with all the accessory corps services.'[2] The Canadian corps was distinctive in its stability and leadership, with some realistic expectation that there could be a high standard of training throughout the corps. It also had outstanding leadership, first in the British General Byng and then in the Canadian General Currie. Furthermore, it was able to draw on the logistical support of the British. This meant more casualties, as most Canadians were front-line soldiers, but a clearer focus on raising performance in the front line. Particularly notable was the continuity and quality of the artillery. Haig was to write after the great German offensives of March–April 1918 that he had no real fears about defeat because he still had the Canadian Corps in reserve.

Canadian Armada arriving at Plymouth on 14 October 1914. Thirty-six Canadian transports carrying 32,000 men ... with unforeseen, indeed, incredible speed.

Folkestone, Kent

In February the Canadians moved to France and also to a permanent base in Folkestone. Folkestone and the adjacent camp of Shorncliffe were where all new Canadian drafts were trained from 1915. There were scores of wooden huts stretching across to Sandling station and down towards Hythe and Folkestone became a temporary home for thousands of Canadians. The trenches used for training are still visible near Sandling station. The Canadian soldiers were paid three times more than the British and their presence created a boom for the publicans and shopkeepers of Folkestone, where the population rose from 10,000 pre-war to 100,000, many of them Canadians. They went through an intensive training programme. A young artilleryman, Harold Innis (later Canada's most distinguished economic historian), joined as a volunteer rather than wait to be conscripted into the infantry: 'no place for a man if he wants to come back alive.' For some four months at Shorncliffe in early 1917 he applied himself diligently to learning the mechanics of musketry drill, signalling, laying telephone wire and gun drills with wagons and 18-pounders. He was adopted by a certain Miss Vickery, a 'jolly old maid [...] Well furnished house, bread very thin, chicken, fruit and custard, chocolates'.[3] The Canadians were popular in the local community.

The Australians

The Australian Imperial Force (A.I.F.) arrived in France in May 1916, after experience at Gallipoli and in Egypt. The Australians arrived via Marseilles rather than the UK and never established as large a permanent base in the UK as the Canadians did. There were high casualties on the Somme, at Mouquet Farm in 1916 and then at Bullecourt in 1917. They were then out of the front line for six months but returned to a record of outstanding success in 1918. They were the pioneers at Hamel in July, working with tanks in the prelude to the German Army's black day, which was to come at the Battle of Amiens three weeks later on 8 August 1918. With experience, intensive training and strong leadership, the Australian Corps came to be the Allied answer to Ludendorff's stormtroopers. As Monash recorded, the year 1918 brought out 'the transcendent military virtues of the Australian infantryman, his bravery, his battle discipline, his absolute reliability, his individual resource, his initiative and endurance'. He later wrote: 'The secrets of success of the Australian open fighting lay in the extraordinary vigour, judgement and team work which characterised the many hundreds of little platoon battles.'[4] Furthermore, he prided himself on a low level of casualties: 'During the 100 days, wastage – killed or wounded – was 70 men per division per day. Even during the period of sedentary trench warfare losses had averaged 40 per division per day.'

In the 100 days at the end of the war, the Australians accounted for 9 per cent of the Allied armies, but took 23 per cent of the prisoners and 21 per cent of the territory. Their captives included many horses. During the visit of the King in August 1918, 'His Majesty was particularly interested in the German transport horses, expressing the hope that they would soon learn the Australian language.'[5] They also captured many Germans. A German battalion commander commented on a mass surrender in September 1918:

> Well you see they are dreadfully afraid of the Australians, so they are of the tanks. But when they saw both of them coming, they thought it was high time to throw up their hands.[6]

Horseferry Road, London

The A.I.F. had an administrative headquarters in Horseferry Road. The buildings were formerly used as a Methodist training school and have

Aussies living it up in London. A Dinkum
Aussie on Blighty leave.

A Canadian in the mud of Salisbury
Plain. Not everybody was so cheerful.

since been demolished to make way for an office block. The Australian
High Commission was able to occupy some of its new Australia House
in the Aldwych. Many Australians came to London on leave, as there
was, of course, no possibility of home leave. They also had camps on
the edge of Salisbury Plain at Codford and Sutton Veny, where training
was carried out by the diminishing number of drafts. This was the last
of the all-volunteer armies after conscription was accepted in Britain
and Canada but rejected in Australia. The link between the military
high command in France under General Currie and the Australian
prime minister was supplied by the journalist Keith Murdoch, father
of Rupert Murdoch. There was contact with Australian Prime Minister
Billy Hughes, who was resident in the UK for much of 1918.

Codford, Wiltshire

The badge on Lambs Down near Codford dates from 1917.[7] The Australian brigade commander wanted to leave a mark on the English

19. View near Sutton Veny camp.

20. Australian soldiers examining the ancient walls of Old Sarum. (Visits were organised by the Y.M.C.A.)

21. Codford village in the snow.

22. Troops leaving Codford camp for return to Australia, April 1919.

Scenes in Wiltshire near Codford and Sutton Veny. Australians were side-lined to the Wyllie Valley for hell-raising.

countryside, and gazing out of the window of his headquarters in Stockton House, he came up with the idea of carving the rising sun badge on the chalk hillside: 'proudly worn in two world wars and an integral part of the Digger tradition!' The initial work was carried out by the 13th Training Battalion Australian Imperial Force (A.I.F.). The badge was then embedded with green, brown and clear beer bottles in order to make it shine as if bronze, like the badge on the Australian uniform.

Maintaining the badge became the focus of punishment parades and, as a result, the spur on which it was carved was known as 'Misery Hill'. The bottles sank into the chalk but the carving is still there and visible from the A36 road in the Wylye Valley. The village of Codford has an ANZAC cemetery with ninety graves, including three Australian graves that are not on the usual Commonwealth War Graves model but were designed and built by comrades, a feature that makes the little cemetery rather rare. For example, there is a fine headstone that reads 'In loving memory of my comrade No. 1879 Cpl A.J. Button A.I.F. killed Nov 23rd 1916', with the name 'J.H. Brown 61 battalion' at the foot of the stone.

The contributions of the Canadian and Australian contingent supplied the narrow margin for victory:

Since the old armies were no longer of high combat value the British on the left used fresh Canadians and Australians with two American divisions, as shock troops while on the right of the giant pincer movement the French used the Americans. The French armies in the centre advanced over territory which fell to them as a result of the successful offensives made by the allies on the flanks. The Germans had few shock troops left and were compelled to submit. The war went to the side with the last battalions but the last battalions of value were non-European – a whisper of the future in 1945.[8]

This may be unfair to some of the British divisions, such as the 46th East Midland Division, with its assault on the Hindenburg Line, but it certainly reflected the Australian experience of the apparent unwillingness of French divisions on their flanks to make any advance.

The Americans

Before the declaration of war in April 1917 there were individual American volunteers fighting with the British Army and rather more with the French. There was a contribution by the Society of Friends of ambulance units to the French Army around Verdun – successor to the volunteer ambulance corps that had assisted during the Franco-Prussian War forty-five years earlier – but the largest organised contribution was from Harvard and Johns Hopkins Medical Schools. Starting from a base in Paris at the American Hospital in Neuilly, there were six American hospitals attached to the British forces, with staff from the old Yankee and Anglophile universities of New England and the East Coast. The leader was the neurosurgeon Harvey Cushing, who later published a diary with some acerbic comments, but a generally positive view of the RAMC. (He was a pioneer, not least in drawing a picture of the inside of the skull of an American Army chief of staff, General Leonard Wood, during a successful operation for removal of a brain tumour in 1908.[9]) Cushing went on to join the RAMC as head of neurosurgery and he was part of a vital American contribution in the medical services, which included the expansion of orthopaedics as a speciality, improved treatment for shock and an essential battalion of medical officers. The visit of Arthur Balfour to the US (the first official visit by a senior British minister since Independence) led to the call for American doctors to serve as battalion medical officers – some 1,200 doctors answered it. After the heavy RAMC casualties, half of the battalion MOs by late 1917 were Americans.[10]

The first active contribution was at sea, with the arrival of a flotilla of American destroyers at Queenstown in Ireland on 7 May 1917 and

GETTING READY FOR SEA
American destroyers at Queenstown.

DEPTH CHARGES
Arranged on board American destroyer in readiness for immediate use.

American destroyers at Queenstown. They were there within weeks.

of a squadron of dreadnoughts, which joined the Grand Fleet at Scapa Flow. The American Army (under General John Pershing) in France held back from integration with the British or French armies, in order to form a distinct national force, but no such inhibitions affected the US Navy. By the autumn of 1917 both the destroyers and the dreadnoughts were fully integrated with the Allied forces. The dreadnought squadron was under the command of Admiral Hugh Rodman, the 'Kentucky Admiral'[11] and included the USS *Texas*, which is the last surviving First World War dreadnought, now moored at San Jacinto State Park in Texas. The American dreadnoughts set out to learn the Royal Navy's signalling codes and to master the treacherous navigation and weather around the Pentland Firth with success. In 1918 the American naval contribution was extended to laying 100,000 mines from Inverness to Norway. All this was under the leadership of the Assistant Secretary of the Navy, who was living in the UK for several months in 1918, Franklin D. Roosevelt.

Liverpool, Lancashire

The first 'doughboys' arrived at Liverpool in June 1917 and camped out in Stanley Park – between Liverpool and Everton football grounds. They brought to the local area the game of baseball, still commemorated by photographs in The Elm Tree pub in Aintree. During 1917 and early 1918, 700,000 Americans passed through Liverpool. Most went by train to Southampton and then on to France. Some stayed for special training with the RAMC in Blackpool or with the Machine Gun Corps in Grantham. The 'Tommies from heaven' (in Beatrice Webb's phrase), who came from all over the US, brought hope.[12] Before the conscripts came the state National Guards with the Rainbow Division – so-called from the mix of National Guards from different states. The British had to get used to accents from the Bronx, the Deep South and the Mid-West, as well as the more familiar accents from New England. There was shock at the racial segregation. The Mid-West contribution was particularly notable, with a permanent legacy, not only in the presidency of an artillery captain called Harry S. Truman, but in the main First World War memorial and museum, which is now in Kansas City. Pershing, like Truman, was also from the state of Missouri. After the German Spring Offensive, the greatly increased flow of troops was mainly shipped direct to France to save time, although still in British-owned and British-crewed ships. Leave camps were organised in south-east France, behind the lines held by the Americans. The British

General Pershing arriving in Liverpool on June 8 1917 (he kept his best line for Paris: *Lafayette, nous voici*) welcomed by the Guard of Honour from the Royal Welsh Fusiliers, including a goat in the background, regiment of Graves, Sassoon and my father.

population saw rather less of the Americans. However, there was still a large official presence in London, as well as four divisions still fighting with the British Army around Ypres. The British were often resented for their superior ways – but envied for the efficiency of their weapons. It was a source of regret to the American soldier that he had to make do with the Hotchkiss machine gun rather than the Vickers-Maxim.

Other Allies

The New Zealand Division did not form an ANZAC force and was less independent than the Australian contingent: its base in the UK was on Salisbury Plain. It was in the Second World War that New Zealand troops played a central role in the Desert War and Italian campaign, helped by inspiring leadership from the First World War veteran,

Sir Bernard Freyberg. The worst Western Front experience for the New Zealanders was at Passchendaele in 1917. South African forces also fought in the battle – a labour corps of black South Africans stayed on – and has a fine memorial at Delville Wood, but after 1916 it was withdrawn to East Africa. Some 70,000 workers, mainly from North China, were also recruited as a labour corps[13] and came to France via Folkestone. Many stayed on after the war to clear shells.

Brighton, Sussex; The Chattri Memorial

The Indian Corps made a crucial contribution, arriving 'across the dark waters' in time for the first Battle of Ypres in 1914.[14] The Indians also fought at the Battle of Neuve Chapelle in 1915. Some of the wounded were treated in the Royal Pavilion at Brighton and a funeral pyre was set up on the South Downs to cremate the bodies of the Hindus and Sikhs in accordance with their religion, with the cemetery at Woking. Difficulties with climate and shortage of drafts then led to redeployment to Mesopotamia. The inscription on the Chattri memorial reads in English, Hindi, Urdu and Punjabi:

> To the memory of all Indian soldiers who gave their lives for the King-Emperor in the Great War, this monument, erected on the site of the funeral pyre where Hindus and Sikhs who died in hospital at Brighton passed through the fire, is in grateful admiration and brotherly love dedicated.

Notes

1 Schreiber, S., *Shock Army of the British Empire*, Praeger/Greenwood, 1997.
2 Monash, J., *The Australian Victories in France* in 1918, Hutchinson, n.d.
3 Gwyn, *Tapestry of War Harper*, 1992, pp. 363–8.
4 Monash, J., loc. cit.
5 Ibid.
6 Bean, C.E.W., *Official History of Australia in the War of 1914–18*, Vol. III, Angus and Robertson, 1929, p. 159.
7 Wyeth, R., loc. cit.
8 Ryan, *Petain the Soldier*, Yoseloff, 1969.
9 Fulton, J.F., *Harvey Cushing: A Biography*, Blackwell, 1946, p. 311.
10 Chapin, *The Lost Legion*, Springfield, Mass., 1926.
11 Rodman, H., *Yarns of a Kentucky Admiral*, Martin Hopkinson, 1929.
12 Webb, B., *Our Partnership*, Longman 1948.
13 Summerskill, M., *China on the Western Front*, London, 1982.
14 Donovan, Tom, 'The Chattri', *Journal of the Indian Military Historical Society*, Summer 2009, Vol. 26, No. 2., pp. 53–65.

3

The Munitions Surprise

The Lloyd George Push and Go

'There is a path which no fowl knoweth and which the vulture's eye
hath not seen.'
Job, 28.7 (sampler above Lloyd George's bed in 10 Downing Street)

For the first two years after the Battle of the Marne in 1914 the British
Army was on the defensive. In the whole period there were only three
short offensives lasting a few days. From 1 July 1916 onwards the
British forces launched the 'greatest strategic surprise in history' – the
141-day offensive of Kitchener's Army on the Somme.[1] As Ludendorff
admitted much later:

> On the Somme the enemy's powerful artillery, assisted by excellent
> aeroplane observation and fed with enormous supplies of
> ammunition, had kept down our own fire and destroyed our artillery.
> The defence of our infantry has become so flabby that the massed
> attacks of the enemy always succeeded. Not only did our morale
> suffer, but in addition to fearful wastage in killed and wounded we
> lost a large number of prisoners and much material.[2]

The Western Front is usually envisaged as a trench system a few miles
wide, but behind the trenches was a support system that stretched
back through the zone of the armies to supply routes, and then back
to the national territories. In the first phase, from 1915–16, the
main British effort was in shell production. The driving force in this
was the personal leadership of David Lloyd George as Minister of

Munitions from 5 June 1915. A network of engineering plants in British cities was set up for milling shell cases. Massive new plants were built for producing explosive and filling shells on greenfield sites, linked by intensive use of the railway network between factories and down to the ports. The shells were made to fit any gun according to calibre. The shell and projectile plants made the casings, the explosives plants milled the new mix of Amatol (expensive TNT and ammonium nitrate) and the filling plant added the propellant, the component fuse and gaine (a small charge on cable leading from nose to explosives) and the payload. The filling plant turned a steel container into a deadly weapon.

The military surprise depended on a social surprise. The great innovation was the role of women munitions workers in milling, making explosives and filling shells. The male workers were doing more traditional jobs in making shell casings and maintenance work. The work done by the women was 'mainly unskilled but in varying degree dangerous'.[3] It was especially unpleasant for the 'canaries' – so-called because of skin-yellowing caused by exposure to TNT – a problem much reduced in time by effective management. Later, however, came unresolved problems of sickness and disability from the production of mustard gas. However, there were compensations in pay (which was two or three times higher than before the war) and in the sense of making a vital contribution, as well as an active social life.[4] Women migrated from smaller towns to work in the munitions plants[5] and the risks were in fact rather less than expected – some 300 deaths from plant explosions in making some 100 million shells. The munitions plants turned out to be safer than the pre-war cotton industry.

The Lloyd George Phase

The Ministry of Munitions built and managed massive new plants for making explosives. These had a royal title, 'His Majesty's Explosives Factories', compared to the 'National Factories' for shell making. They were munitions fortresses laid out on greenfield sites stretching over hundreds of acres; they had high perimeter fences and searches were carried out every day for matches by women policemen, who were employed to guard the mainly female workforce. The shifts were long but conditions were good, in fact the best ever offered by employers in the UK, apart from a few sites such as Rowntree's in York and the Lever Brothers in Port Sunlight. In time there was recreation and sport, with a particular speciality in women's football (thriving

*From One of Our Girls
To One of Our Boys*

To..

....

Photograph of Sender
may be pasted on this
space.

From..

....

Ministry of Munitions sponsored book, 1917:
'From one of our girls to one of our boys'–
with room for a photo.

then but banned by the FA after the war). In a few places there was purpose-built accommodation, most extensive at Gretna Green, and in others free, or subsidised, transport to work.

The munitions fortresses were built near rail links and water sources, against a background of low hills to contain explosions. The plants drew on the experience of deep mining in South Africa. Production of explosives rose sharply and quality improved, which led to complaints about dud shells on the Somme (imported from the United States) being replaced by statements of appreciation. In the factories accidents were few. There was much greater danger when, in order to increase production, explosives were made in converted premises in urban areas, as in Silvertown, East London. On 19 January 1917 an explosion killed sixteen staff and fifty-three local residents. A few months later, on 13 June at Ashton-under-Lyne in Lancashire, a TNT plant constructed in a former cotton mill exploded, killing twenty-four employees and nineteen local residents, including a young boy hit by falling glass in a covered swimming pool.

The Second Phase: Churchill as Minister of Munitions

The shell factories were only the first phase of the munitions drive. By 1917 the British Army had more shells than it could use; indeed, the use of massed artillery was beginning to generate deadly side effects in impassable mud on ground torn up by shellfire in the Passchendaele (Third Ypres) campaign. The munitions programme had to switch to develop a new range of weapons to assist the army to break the deadlock – machine guns, aircraft, tanks and gas. This phase saw Churchill as Minister of Munitions, after the 'shell phase' led by Lloyd George. The munitions world became less of a self-contained empire, producing its own materials – it had to fight for priority with the Royal Navy and others in the war effort.

The range of new weapons were more complex and less suited to central planning. Correlli Barnett has chronicled the woeful record of British industry during and after the Second World War in *The Audit of War*[6],but in the First World War the record was very different. British industry adjusted to produce a new range of weapons: 100 million shells, 22,000 aircraft and over 3,000 tanks. By the end of the war it was equipping the American as well as the British forces. In the first two years there was dependence on the munitions produced in the United States and Canada – some 78 million shells overall – but by the end of the war the roles were reversed, with the British munitions industry showing stronger performance in production of weapons, tanks and aircraft.

The munitions drive had a great impact on attitudes and changed political debate. It served as the template for the government-led stimulus which was to be so often advocated in the future. Clement Attlee (later Labour prime minister) devoted his maiden speech in 1922 to the programme:

> Why was it that in the War we were able to find employment for everyone? It was simply that the government controlled the purchasing power of the nation. They said what things should be produced: they said, 'we must have munitions of war; we must have machine guns; we must have saddles'. They took by means of taxation and by methods of loan, control of the purchasing power into making those things that were necessary for winning the war. This is what we are demanding shall be done in time of peace. As the nation was organised for war and death so it can be organised for peace and life if we have the will for it.[7]

The programme had actually depended on the resources created by market activity over the previous decades. The success of the programme depended on local initiative as much as central planning. The munitions programme had a profound effect on economic and political attitudes for the next forty years. The success at the time was real but the transferability to peacetime conditions was vastly exaggerated.

It is hoped that this examination of the main sites will encourage local searches for the 218 National Factories that were on the Ministry of Munitions register. The full list with addresses is available in the *Official History of the Ministry of Munitions*, Vol. VIII, pp. 246–55.

Woolwich Arsenal, London

The original munitions fortress was at the Woolwich Arsenal in south-east London and this remained the hub for the munitions effort throughout the war. The Arsenal dated from Tudor times and had been active in developing artillery and explosives from the 1700s onwards. The guns and shells were taken down the estuary by barge to Shoeburyness on the point of Essex (Southend-on-Sea) for testing. In 1914 Woolwich already had a high wall (much of it still there today) with a large gate and guards. In the ten years before 1914 there were arguments about its capacity and costs as well as a period of redundancies, but from 5 August 1914 there was rapid expansion. The role was vital in the first stages of the war when the Arsenal was filling 90 per cent of shells. Across the whole war it filled 20 million shells, as well as making 57 million fuses and 1.7 billion rounds of small arms ammunition.

The Gatehouse of Woolwich Arsenal, the hub of the whole munitions system.

Munitions worker at the Arsenal, probably at the start of a twelve-hour shift.

In the first period many of the workers were working ninety-six hours a week, seven days a week, for many weeks without a break. The one compensation was that wage levels could be excellent – with the retention of pre-war agreements on bonuses some were earning as much as £10 a week, which is £1,000 in today's terms. The Arsenal also carried out design work and specialised tool making for other factories – for example, most of the inspection gauges and drawings used by other factories. The shell dimensions set at Woolwich had to be followed throughout and plants were inspected by inspectors from Woolwich.

At Woolwich this expansion of 3.4 million square feet was achieved with great difficulty and did not produce a well organised site:

> Layouts were poor and internal transport a nightmare. Many of the shops were unsuitable for modern plant, badly lighted and ill ventilated. The efficient siting of the new shops was difficult and sometimes impossible, and the congestion which increased as the tide of war advanced made economic management more and more of a Herculean task.[8]

The Arsenal produced its prodigious output by employing some 72,000 people by the end of the war, compared to 11,000 in 1913 – far more than any other munitions plant. Some of the new workers were accommodated in the specially built Well Hall estate in Eltham but most came by train or ferry.[9] The Arsenal has gone but the site has been well restored and is now open to the public. The former pier for loading shells in transit to Shoeburyness can be seen at the end of the new housing development.

Oldbury, Staffordshire

This was the first purpose-built plant for TNT and the first to be designed and managed by K.B. Quinan, whose services were lent by the de Beers Consolidated Mining Company. Quinan arrived in England on 5 January 1915 and work on the TNT site began on 8 January. By November the factory had reached its full output.

The site was next to an existing chemical plant and close to Langley Green Station on the Great Western Railway. The plant included a laboratory, which developed a new continuous process and 'enabled the original installation to increase its output fivefold with only slight structural alterations'.[10] However, the site, with a canal on one side, was too cramped for further expansion and the area also gained a less-than-enviable reputation for strikes. The search was on for sites both green and removed from the trades unions.

Gretna, Dumfries and Galloway

The most ambitious new build by the Ministry of Munitions was at Gretna Green, an area remote from large cities but within reach of the labour force of Clydeside.[11] This was a massive plant, which ran across the English/Scottish border in a series of linked buildings 9 miles long. It was built by Quinan on a greenfield site, safe from the distractions of hostelries and pubs. Planned output was 3,300 tons a month. Nitroglycerine and nitrocotton were kneaded into a paste, which Sir Arthur Conan Doyle, the creator of Sherlock Holmes, called 'The Devil's Porridge' during a visit in 1916. 'The factory was divided into several areas. At Dornoch there was the glycerine distillery (1,201 acres). The paste was then dispatched eastwards to the Mossband area (1,381 acres). Here it is made into cordite.'[12] In this area were eight units or 'ranges', widely dispersed for the sake of safety. There was an electric power station on a 10-acre site at Rigg, and reservoirs and filters covered 14 acres: 'The above were all fenced areas patrolled by the military guard and used for factory operations.'[13] The plant was a great success, producing 56,000 tons of explosives during the war without fatal accident. The cordite went to the filling plants along the main

Workers from the Gretna Green munitions factory, which was 9 miles long and designed by an explosive expert from South Africa.

London and Glasgow railway, which passed through the eastern end of the site.

The Ministry of Munitions also used the Women's Police Service (WPS) to search workers at its factories. At Gretna, near Carlisle, over 9,000 women were employed to produce munitions and 150 members of the WPS had the responsibility of searching them when they entered and left the factory. The maximum number of workers in the plant was 19,772 in October 1917, with women 70 per cent of the total. Most of the men were employed in plant maintenance and internal transport while the women worked up The Devil's Porridge. The plant was unique in terms of the size of the investment in housing. Two townships were built at Gretna in the central part of the plant area and at Eastrigg on the west. Each township, planned by Raymond Unwin, designer of garden cities, had its own church, schools, public halls, post offices and shops. The cost was large – the plant and housing together accounted for a capital expenditure of £9.25 million, about as much as was spent on some twenty other factories together. Today, the houses at Eastrigg, converted from hostels into flats, are occupied and the shops and post office still stand – by far the most extensive survival from that period. There is also an excellent small museum run by local volunteers called The Devil's Porridge.

Queensferry, Flintshire

This was a much smaller factory than the Gretna Green plant, with 298 acres on a narrow site between the River Dee and the hills in North Wales, but for its size it was one of the most expensive, with a capital expenditure of £4 million. The cost was the result of the complex processes carried out there, starting with the manufacture of nitrocellulose (gun cotton), which was turned into cordite at Gretna Green. It also produced TNT, and by 1918 was producing 700 tons per week, which made it by far the largest producer. It was a chemical works rather than a works for finished shells and was one of the most sophisticated chemical works of the time. The workforce was smaller than at Gretna and Chilwell: in October 1918 there were 3,749 employees, of whom 42 per cent were women. Most of the workers travelled in by train from North Wales and Chester. Compared to Chilwell, the women who worked at Queensferry seemed to have a wider age range, with some older workers, and some came from a rural background in one of the poorest areas of the country. A housing development was built at Mancot, although on a much smaller scale than at Gretna or Woolwich. The plant seems to have been relatively safe, with only four lives lost; however, injuries and burns were much more common, with 12,500 reported in 1917–18.

There was a strong team of chemists working at the plant. One exceptionally talented member was the young Cyril Hinshelwood, who, after three years of service at Queensferry, passed his Oxford BA and Master's Degree in one year and later won the Nobel Prize.[14]

The factory was in an area with a special expertise in chemicals – Manchester and Cheshire. It edged onto the Hawarden estate of the great peacemaker William Ewart Gladstone. This is still an industrial site. Some buildings remain from the plant and there is more housing in Mancot.

Pembrey, Wales

The explosives factory in Pembrey was built on the site of an early failed Nobel dynamite factory on the South Wales coast, a few miles from the birthplace of poet Dylan Thomas. A line of sand hills inland supplied the safety barrier and there were good transport links with the Great Western Railway nearby. This was the only large plant to be located some distance into Wales (with Queensferry on the English border), with over 400 working buildings for explosives production. The plant was established for supplying water, electric light, power and steam. Daily water consumption was 4 million gallons and steam was generated from thirty-three boilers, which produced 5 million pounds of steam a day. There were no public services in the remote sand dunes and caves of the site near the sea and no accommodation; workers had to come in on free trains, mainly from Llanelli.

National Filling Factories

National Filling Factories were funded by the Ministry of Munitions, but most were not directly managed by it. The largest was at Chilwell, which produced half the heavy shells used in the war. This was a purpose-built fortress on an isolated site with its own guards; however, other filling factories were smaller, using existing factory sites. These plants were run on an agency basis by private firms and were much more like ordinary factories than the explosives plants. They drew their workforce from local communities and there were no special arrangements for transport and recreation, although there were medical services and precautions against contamination. They relied heavily on the rail network, which brought them both the supplies of explosives and the shell cases.

Chilwell, Nottinghamshire

This was the factory where most of the heavy shells filled for the Western Front became live. It was the one factory that was so vital to the war effort that a whole replacement plant (never fully used) was built at Hereford. The large industrial complex was built on 208 acres of greenfield 5 miles south of Nottingham with, as usual, low hills in the background and close to a main railway line. To the north was a mixing and milling plant on a continuous process capable of producing 1,000 tons of explosive a week, with equipment borrowed from the sugar industry in East London. The shells were filled and stored to the south. The factory was designed by Lord Chetwynd, an extreme example of Lloyd George's 'men of push and go', hostile to any effort to hold him back with a 'bridle of red tape'.[15] As a former Deputy

3.—*Interior view of the Filled Shell Store—Building 157. Area of the building 8½ acres, holding approximately 700,000 filled shells.*

4.—*Women at war—Chilwell girls dressed for filling shells.*

Chilwell filled shell store and its women workers.

The filled shell store building today – still with wooden blocks on the floor to prevent sparks.

The last First World War telephone pole for Chilwell; the line to the Ministry.

Sheriff of Greene County, Texas, he brought American experience to bear. He planned the factory on half a sheet of paper and when the Treasury wired 'must see plans as soon as completed', he wired back: 'factory half built – will send plans as soon as completed.'[16] The factory was built in six months using 6,000 tons of steel and 10 million bricks.

Chilwell began filling shells in February 1916, in time for the Battle of the Somme. It employed 6,000 men and 4,000 women. No housing was built and workers came in by train. Many of the women were former lace workers, whose earnings were two and half times what they had been in the lace industry: 30s a week compared to 12s a week. 'Work at the filling factories was marked by two characteristics; it was unskilled, and it was all, to a greater or lesser degree, according to the nature of the work, dangerous.'[17] The sheer volume and flow of explosives made Chilwell the most dangerous of all.

All went well for the first two years. The canteen made sure that all women in the danger buildings had two square meals a day, with meat, vegetables, eggs and bacon for 10d a day. The Reverend Walter Chetwynd, Lord Chetwynd's brother, 'turned his collar round' and went to Nottingham market to buy forty sheep and eight bullocks a week. The plant had football teams and a band. The plant seemed safe from air raids, although a Zeppelin one night in 1916 'hunted up and down the Trent Valley looking for it'. Another kind of disaster struck on 1 July 1918 when an explosion of 8 tons of amatol destroyed the mixing mill and killed 134 people. Many could not be identified and were buried in a mass grave in Attenborough Churchyard. Next morning the workers were back to filling shells. The disaster was variously blamed on sabotage by rabid socialists and on spontaneous combustion after a long period of hot running. Early bids to win the factory the title of Chilwell VC did not come to fruition.

Chilwell is still a Ministry of Defence (MoD) site known as Chetwynd Barracks. The filled shell store is visible from the local road and the graves in Attenborough Churchyard are still there but in need of restoration. There is a memorial to the fallen inside the camp.

National Shell Factories

These were the least controlled of the munitions plants, with the fewest special arrangements and the greatest variation in size and organisation. A few were large, as in Leeds, but others, such as the shell factory in Rochdale, only employed 366 people, compared to the 70,000 at the Woolwich Arsenal. The first plants were called National Shell

Factories, which made the smaller shells used at the start of the war. Later came a sub-type of National Projectile Factories, which made larger shells. The labour force was much more like the pre-war labour force in many of these factories, which were run by well-established local engineering firms. The weight of shells in the projectile factories was less favourable to women's employment, together with local resistance to dilution. These factories had a past quite unlike the greenfield sites and they were also more likely to be sited in smaller towns. They often formed co-operative networks, especially in the south-west.

Leeds, Yorkshire

This was the first National Shell Factory, one built with less fuss and dislocation, and the one that did the most varied work. It was the product of a team effort by local managers rather than by the big names such as Lord Chetwynd at Chilwell and K.B. Quinan at Gretna Green. It was linked to the nearby Leeds shell-making plants, thus minimising transport problems, and produced 24.5 million shells over the war period. The site was on the outskirts of Leeds on 400 acres described as 'a city within a city'.

The gate leading to the National Shell Factory at Crossgates in Leeds. Yorkshire made the money go a long way.

The first plant was a filling plant, but in 1916 it was decided to add a mill for making amatol. There was a 10 kilovolt overhead line to provide temporary electricity, a boiler house and heating plant and water-main supplying 200 gallons a day. The plant was notable for the speed of construction and low cost of extensions. In 1916, a small plant was installed on the site for making gun-ammunition boxes at a cost of £260,000 and the total investment on the site was £813,200 – compared to £2.2 million at Chilwell and £9.2 million at Gretna Green.[18] Yorkshire made the taxpayers' money go a long way!

The factory was also notable for its unrelenting search for increased productivity. A workforce of 16,000 in mid-1916 was reduced to 13,000 by early 1917 with a new bonus scheme, and output rose: 'The administration department was efficiently equipped with electric payroll, addition and calculating machines – with the large accounts department being divided into 13 sections.'[19]

The shells went to the ports by train, where heavy trainloads were handled, increasing from 150 trucks a day in 1916 to over 600 trucks a day in the autumn of 1918. The total monthly tonnage of materials being transported in and out of the plant was 100,000 tons.

The plant employed 12,150 women and 1,165 men in 1917–18. No special housing was built but the North Eastern Railway operated thirty-eight special trains every twenty-four hours, known as 'Barnbow Specials'. There were three canteens and the kitchens were equipped with the most up-to-date appliances, including electric cookers, potato peelers etc. There were 120 cows on site to provide milk, and pigs were fed on kitchen waste. Additionally, there was a rest room, a surgery, two dentists and even tennis courts. A barbed-wire fence enclosed the whole site, patrolled by police guards. The plant had one major accident on the night of 5 December 1916, when thirty-five women lost their lives. Local residents at the time witnessed 'crowds of workers, many with yellowed faces, rushing along Manston Lane, all in a state of great distress'.[20] There was a second accident in March 1917, with two killed, and a third on 31 March 1918, with three fatalities.

The site was, until recently, still making tanks, and the railway line to the south can still be seen. There is a fading memorial to those killed in the explosions in the centre of a roundabout in Crossgates.

Liverpool, Lancashire

The city showed a remarkable record of local initiative in adapting existing buildings. This started with a site in Haymarket in the city

The Cunard Shell Works in Liverpool.

FIRST 6 & 8 SHELLS
MANUFACTURED IN GREAT BRITAIN
BY LADY OPERATORS
AT
CUNARD S.S Cos SHELL WORKS
RIMROSE Rd   1915.

Some of the first shells.

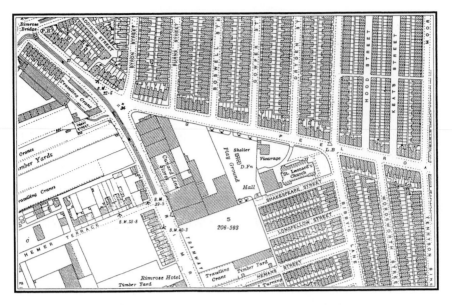

Map of Rimrose Road.

centre, which had been an agricultural produce market. The original
plant of sixty lathes was expanded to 350. Next came the offer from
the Cunard Steamship Company to contribute a site in Rimrose Road,
which had been a warehouse for ship fitting. Other sites followed at
Edge Lane, on the site of the Liverpool International Exhibition of
1887, and at the tramways depot in Lambeth Road. The four sites in
Liverpool produced 3.1 million shells at a capital cost of £266,000.
Some 70–80 per cent of the employees were women: 'The extent of
female dilution was high.'[21]

Shell cases were transported to the rail sidings in trucks. A small
factory making gauges in Bootle were added to the shell factories – the
only such factory outside Woolwich – and an explosives plant at Lith-
erland. This plant, adapted from the local chemical works of Brother-
ton's, was less successful than the greenfield sites and most of the shells
would have been filled at Chilwell.

Liverpool supplied a remarkable example of munitions activity at
the heart of an urban area, with the main Leeds plant situated on the
edge of the city, on a greenfield site. The four Liverpool shell plants
were close to housing and, in the case of the Rimrose Road plant, only
yards from the street. In a city with experience of dangerous and frag-
ile cargoes, the safety record was impeccable – there were no fatalities
in making 3 million shells.

Birtley, County Durham: The Birtley Belgians

The most unexpected development of all was the Projectile Factory at Birtley, County Durham, entirely organised and staffed by Belgian ex-servicemen. There were very few women employed; in fact, by October 1918 there were 3,826 men and no women. The plant was highly efficient, producing 2 million shells, including many of the heavy 60-pounder shrapnel type.

Birtley became a Belgian enclave known as Elisabethville, with its own family housing, schools and shops. At the end of the war most were repatriated. The site, which is on the main road south of Gateshead, continued to be an industrial site, first for Caterpillar then for Komatsu.

Co-ordination

Perhaps the greatest surprise of all was the extraordinarily efficient co-ordination of the 218 national factories and the many hundreds of private contractors. This involved planning for delivery of components to the filling factories where fuses and gaines were fitted. Even before then, there was co-ordination to be done between the shell factories and contract makers of components. Each shell had forty components and each rifle over 100. The system worked smoothly and had to pass extreme tests for increasing production at times of military crisis. The King himself praised the efforts of munitions works in replacing the huge losses of guns and shells in the 1918 German offensive within six weeks. Such rushed programmes raised the risk. The worst explosions at Chilwell and Ashton-under-Lyne came on the afternoon of a hot summer's day, at a time of major offensives, with a problem of inadequate cleaning and maintenance of pipes.

Even the business of sorting and loading components and then shells was very complex, and is still by far the largest industrial effort mounted in the UK; in the Churchill phase came the new challenge of more complex equipment and components. Great, too, was the challenge of transport between all the sites; the munitions expansion depended on the railways.

The workers in the shell factories had to learn in a few months skills the arsenals had developed over centuries. As Winston Churchill, in a rather rare tribute to the contribution of women, said:

It is a striking fact that more than nine-tenths, and in many branches more than nine-tenths of the whole manufacture of shells which constitute the foundations, the power and terror of the British artillery, are due to the labour of women – of women who before the war never saw a lathe.[22]

Royal Small Arms Factory, Enfield Lock

This site began to develop after the Napoleonic Wars as a government factory to provide competition to the gun makers in Birmingham. It was expanded during the 1860s, mainly using American machinery to meet the growing demand for rifles: its best-known rifle, the Lee-Enfield, also had American assistance through adaptation by the American, James Paris Lee. The Lee-Enfield rifle was an effective weapon in terms of accuracy, staying power and durability in mud and cold. Every British infantryman had one in the First World War, and for nearly every soldier the weapon meant security and reliability. It was paid a compliment by the Canadians when, in 1915, they threw away their Ross rifles (which jammed after fifty rounds) and picked up Lee-Enfields from fallen British soldiers. The American Army was still using the Lee-Enfield in 1941. It was this rifle that made the fifteen rounds a minute possible. RSA Enfield's location on an island at Enfield Lock, between the River Lea and the Lee navigation, made for problems in expanding production, nor was it easy to get workers to the site.

A number of buildings are still standing on the site, including the machine shop and a small museum, and there is now an Enfield Lock housing estate. Development was only possible because of the lack of ground contamination – a tribute to the care and diligence of the workers since 1816. A row of cottages built after 1816 for the artisans at the Royal Small Arms Factory is still there.

Newcastle, Northumberland

The Armstrong Whitworth plant in Elswick was the largest producer of heavy guns. The company also had a massive shipyard on the Tyne, which built both warships and the new Standard ships, forerunners of the Liberty ship. The production of guns involved an integrated system with forging of the barrels and manufacture of the gun carriages. It involved highly dangerous work, with red-hot metal objects weighing several tons. The molten barrels had to be cooled so as to meet exacting specifications; this was the kind of plant where skilled engineers

Armstrong Whitworth at Elswick, the British answer to Krupps.

made a vital contribution. The quality of British heavy guns and how-itzers was superb.

Birmingham, Warwickshire

Birmingham made its greatest contribution by manufacturing components that could not be made by unskilled labour in the new factories. The production of rifles rose from 135 a week to 2,000 a week in 1917. There were 102 operations in the manufacture of a single rifle cartridge and the limit of accuracy prescribed in nearly all the finished dimensions is within one thousandth of an inch.

Birmingham Council commissioned an excellent history of the city during the war and quoted a visiting American journalist's view of the city in 1918:

> Birmingham, hive of industry where work proceeds to the roar of the furnace, the hiss of escaping steam, the rhythmic throb of the engine, the crash of hydraulic presses, the metallic ring of stamping machines and the clatter of lighter operations as fuse parts are being assembled.

Birmingham Small Arms Company, now an ASDA supermarket. The Lewis gun was made here.

No turn of the kaleidoscope ever produced a more startling change than the total conversion accomplished in Birmingham: jewellers abandoned their craftsmanship for the production of anti-gas apparatus and other war matériel; old-established firms, noted for their art production, which had found a permanent home in most of the museums of the world, turned to the manufacture of an intricate type of hand-grenade; cycle-makers devoted their activities to fuses and shells; world-famous pen makers adapted their machines to the manufacture of cartridge clips; railway-wagon companies came out with artillery wagons, limbers, tanks and aeroplanes; and the chemical works devoted their efforts to the production of deadly TNT. All the people of the city became absorbed in the new national effort.[23]

The Birmingham industry showed great adaptability in war as it had in peace. It even expanded output of one of its peacetime products made in Aston – Houses of Parliament (or 'HP') sauce. This was the people's brown sauce, as opposed to the more upper-class Lea and Perrins Worcester Sauce.

Sheffield, Yorkshire

Firth was an important site in Sheffield, not far from the current Meadowhall shopping centre. The company was the first to use stainless steel and had supplied high-quality steel in the American Civil War. It carried out work jointly with Hadfields, the firm on the adjacent site. Firth made a very important contribution in producing the steel for the British helmet. This was recognised as the best helmet available, as the thickness and quality could stop a bullet, which the German helmet could not. It was estimated that the helmet had saved 50,000 lives and many serious injuries.

The helmet was an idea borrowed from the French Army in 1915 and by the Battle of the Somme Firth had produced a million helmets. The American Army were to wear them in this war and through to 1941.

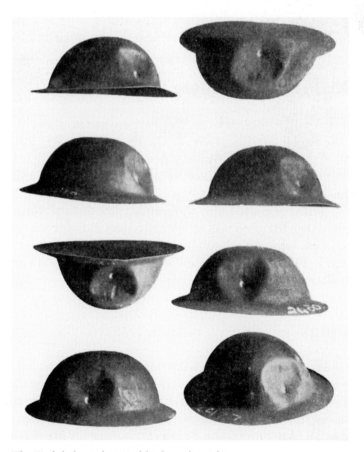

The Firth helmet that could take a direct hit.

Erith and Crayford, Kent

The site in Crayford was occupied by Hiram Maxim, having moved away from the cramped conditions of Hatton Garden in central London. All 12,000 machine guns – known as the Vickers-Maxim – were made here. It was highly regarded for its rate of fire and reliability. Water-cooled, it could fire many more rounds without the barrel distortion that affected the air-cooled French Hotchkiss.

Manufacture was highly complex and skilled. The space was on the marshes, which had only become accessible by rail. Vickers had to sponsor the building of the Barnes Cray Estate to house the workers at the factory. In the last stages of the war the factory also produced long-range bombers, including the Vickers Vimy, which was flown by Alcock and Brown for the first non-stop flight across the Atlantic in June 1919.

A few buildings remain, like the canteen (now used as a municipal headquarters) and the clock tower (surrounded by retail development).

Woolwich, Royal Artillery

The Royal Artillery Barracks at Woolwich was the main headquarters for the Royal Artillery (RA) in the First World War. Across the Common is the old Royal Military Academy ('the Shop') where RA officers continued to be trained even after other training had moved to Sandhurst. In the First World War both the college and the barracks had an expanded role and many thousands went through them.

The trial range for guns was at Shoeburyness in Essex – a range that remained in use long enough to block the building of an estuary airport at Foulness in the 1970s. The main field for training was at Larkhill on Salisbury Plain.

Cambridge

New methods of sound-ranging were developed in France, led by Captain Lawrence Bragg – still the youngest person ever to win the Nobel Prize, at 26, for his work on the structure of crystals. Along with Corporal Tucker he developed new ways of pinpointing enemy artillery using an array of microphones. Bragg carried out his pre-war work at the old Cavendish laboratories in Cambridge.

Notes

1 Germains, V.W., *The Kitchener Armies*, Peter Davis, London, 1930.

2 Ludendorff, E., *War Memoirs*, Longmans, London, p. 267.

3 *Official History of the Ministry of Munitions*, Vol. VIII, Naval and Military Press Reprint, 1922, p. 150.

4 Marwick, A., *Women at War*, Fontana/IWM, 1977. The average wage for women 'before the war' was 11*s*. 7*d*.

5 Walbrook, H.M., *Hove In the Great War*, The Cliftonville Press, 1920, p. 32.

6 Barnett, C., *The Audit of War: The Illusion and Reality of Britain as a Great Nation*, Macmillan, 1986.

7 Harris, K., *Attlee*, Weidenfeld and Nicolson, 1982, p. 59.

8 *Official History of the Ministry of Munitions*, Vol. VIII, 1922, pp. 24–27.

9 Jefferson, E.F.E., *The Woolwich Story 1890–1965*, Instance Printers, Woolwich.

10 *Official History of the Ministry of Munitions*, Vol. VIII, 1922, p. 69.

11 Ibid, pp. 43–7.

12 Ibid, pp. 59.

13 Ibid.

14 Biographical entry for Cyril Hinshelwood, Wikipedia, 2012.

15 Lloyd George, D., *War Memoirs*, Vol. 1, p. 356.

16 Haslam, M.J., 'The Chilwell Story', *RAOC Gazette*, 1982.

17 *Official History of the Ministry of Munitions*, Vol. VIII, 1922, p. 150.

18 Ibid, p. 169.

19 'Barnbow Munitions Factory 1915–18', *The Barwicker*, No. 47, p. 3.

20 *The Barwicker*, p. 6.

21 *Official History of the Ministry of Munitions*, p. 108.

22 Churchill, W.S., *The World Crisis*, Thornton Butterworth, 1923.

23 Brazier, R.H. and Sandford, E., *Birmingham and the Great War, 1914–1919*, Cornish, 1921, p. 123.

The Supply Lifelines

The German front lines were only 100 miles from the national frontier. The British supply lines stretched for hundreds of miles back into the UK and involved a sea crossing and double loading and unloading. Yet there were few complaints about the speed and reliability of deliveries, with very few critical hold-ups at ports. At the beginning there was improvisation, adapting available equipment; later came special trucks (the rectanks) for tanks and other heavy equipment and a new purpose-built port at Richborough.

Logistical competence gave Britain an unexpected success against the expected German advantage of interior lines. Reinforcements of men and munitions could be moved very quickly to the front. The heavy losses after the German 1918 offensives were fully replaced within six weeks, conveying a sense of relentless build-up with unlimited resources.

The logistic success meant security and reliability for the cross-Channel journey. Soldiers with leave permits did not waste their leave on train delays. If they were wounded they could be sure of reliable journeys in well-designed and fully staffed hospital trains and on the way to and from the front there were free services in tearooms, plus currency exchange and postal services. From 1915 onwards the transit conditions were far superior to those in the French Army, helped by the use of volunteers in a way unknown across the Channel. Better logistics made for a sense of security and better morale.

A more general endorsement of the logistics was given by a Royal Artillery battery adjutant:

Yet, whatever may be thought or written today about the tactical and strategic skills, or the lack of it, possessed by our higher command we in France and Flanders in 1917 and 1918 had no complaints about the way in which we were administered. Our medical, transport and supply services had advanced a long way since the days of the Boer and Crimean Wars. We were well fed and clothed; when we were wounded or sick we were admirably looked after; leave was given fairly, regularly and generously; during my time with the BEF there was no shortage of guns or ammunition, motors, maps or indeed of anything. To us it seemed that the vast if at times cumbersome machine worked smoothly, and to us it was the last word in modernity.[1]

The backbone of supply was the railway system. By building a few short link lines, such as a 700yd link between Whetstone on the Great Central Railway and Blaby on the London and North Western Railways main line, it was possible to have a single network with trains working throughout Britain: 'Between Thurso and Penzance or Margate and the Kyle of Lochalsh, all the separate and individual companies were working towards a common objective.'[2]

In fact, at midnight London time on 4 August, exactly one hour after the declaration of war, two-thirds of railway companies and all the larger companies came under state control, as provided for in the Act of 1871. Yet the railways were run by experienced rail managers through control rooms at Manchester, Derby and York, with a central office at 35 Parliament Street in London. For most of the time Herbert Walker of the Southern Railway acted as chairman. It was at his Southern Railway terminus of Waterloo that the finest memorial to the railwaymen was built.

The initial challenge of mobilisation passed smoothly, with 1,200 trains arriving at Southampton. The first message was 'business as usual', yet there were soon pressures to reduce civilian travel, so cheap tickets were suspended. Some of the increased military traffic in goods and equipment was predictable; more unexpected was the shift of material carried by coastal shipping to railways in response to the threats from submarines and mines. The Victorian investment in track and equipment stood up remarkably to this large increase in train frequency and weight. The suspension of coastal shipping threw many hundreds of train-loads of coal and building materials onto the railways. The building of the vast munitions factories added to the pressure. It would have been impossible to change the infrastructure quickly. Without the rail success there would have been a shortage of supplies.

The experienced rail crews were crucial (although many had enlisted, there were enough for safe running). Women workers made a significant contribution as ticket collectors and cleaners but they were excluded from direct work on the trains – not even a shunting engine was driven by a woman. The barrier to mobility or dilution was much greater than those in engineering.

The role of the railways increased further after the spring of 1917 when many locomotives and crew had to be transferred to France, where the engines were painted in large white letters 'R.O.D.' for Railway Operating Division. There were also many miles of new tracks built. Each division needed twenty train-loads of supplies a day and the existing railways, in what had been one of the poorest parts of France, could not stand the strain. The usual troubleshooter, Sir Eric Geddes, was sent to France to sort out the problem.[3] Within six months he had brought about a very significant improvement – but with the effect of causing more strain on the domestic network as a result of sending 100 engines over to France.

By 1917 there were canteens on every station both in the UK and in France. The canteen at Banbury was open from 6 a.m. to midnight throughout the war, staffed by volunteers. Eventually there were purpose-built hospital trains to carry the wounded north from Dover and Southampton.

Commuting to work by train was vital for large munitions sites, which had to draw workers from a wide area. Gretna was the only large plant that built accommodation for the majority of its workers. At Woolwich, Chilwell, Barnbow and Hayes Middlesex, most workers came in by train. The railways took them to work – they also took the shells to the front. Sometimes letters were sent on munitions trains to soldiers near the front.

The war brought the expansion of quiet stations that had been little more than occasional halts before. This was particularly the case around Salisbury Plain, where platforms had to be enlarged rapidly, first for construction workers and then for troops in training. However, such had been the Victorian development of multiple routes between cities that few new lines had to be built, even in remote locations.

The railways had to take far heavier traffic than before, with the weight of shells, heavy guns and, later, tanks. All the heavy loads of building materials for munitions works had to be carried by rail, as the carrying capacity of the expanding number of lorries was too small for long-distance haulage on a limited network of metalled roads.

The new system was a great success, bringing supplies to the front far more quickly than was possible for the German Army, which was affected both by a shortage of freight cars and also the stress of a two-front war with four days required for east–west transfer.

The Gate of Goodbye at Victoria. Families were not allowed past the gate.

The pre-war British railway system had been based on separate companies running services into London termini north of the river. The main system was to the north of the Thames but innovation was south of the river, with the electrification of suburban lines (pioneered by Herbert Walker). Now the links between companies came to be vital, as did the lines across the Thames towards the Channel ports.

Victoria Station, London

As the war expanded the British people came to be a nation on the move. For the first time outside London, thousands of people began to commute to work by train, with soldiers moving to the front or returning on leave. For many it was the first experience of travel outside their home districts. The crossing point between the civilian and the military was very distinct – it was the arch at Victoria Station:

Wives mums and girl-friends would accompany the returning leave men to Victoria. They had to say their farewells at the entrance since they were not allowed on the platform. 'The Gate of Good-bye', the *Illustrated London News* called its famous picture that captured the daily scene of heartbreak, as the men returned to the trenches and the women went home, to start at each knock on the door in case it should mean the dreaded telegram.[4]

Willesden Junction

For passengers there was still a break of journey in London but for freight there were new through-routes on the lines from the munitions works in the North and Midlands to the South in Dover, Folkestone, Newhaven and Southampton. One key route was from the north, switching farther west through Bushbury Junction, near Wolverhampton, Banbury and Basingstoke. Banbury was a vital junction that became even more vital when a large shell-filling plant was built next to the station.[5]

One special problem that emerged quickly was that the main supply routes lay through London and down to the coast, while pre-war developments had led to rail termini north of the Thames. It was essential to devise routes across London all starting from the North London Line. Willesden Junction became the key point where trains from the North and the Midlands joined the line. The main line for heavy freight lay down past Olympia and then over Sands End Bridge in Fulham to a point north of Clapham Junction. The second line was through the Rotherhithe tunnel. Lastly, there was a line that ran past King's Cross and then over what is now a tube line, 'the Metropolitan widened line', to the south. Some traffic avoided London altogether by routing down from Banbury to Basingstoke and then to Newhaven or Southampton.

Trains came down from the north – one an hour at peak times – and then went farther south. Most went past Olympia (then called Addison Road) through Fulham with its railway yards behind Earl's Court and then over Sands End Bridge. The line then went south near Clapham Junction towards Herne Hill and the coast.

The other main route was through the Metropolitan Railway line by King's Cross and then through a tunnel to the coast, but this was limited in the loads that could be carried and the number of carriages. It was used mainly for movement of troops. The third and least used route south went through East London and the Rotherhithe tunnel. This was mainly used by hospital trains, so the West London route though Willesden Junction and Fulham became the main route for munitions trains.

Effective management was, of course, paramount. One of the greatest of the intermediate tier of managers was Herbert Walker, General Manager of the Southern Railway. He worked through control centres that scheduled hundreds of trains a day and had to decide on priorities for

The rail route from Willesden Junction crosses the Thames at Sands End Bridge, Fulham; the main supply route to the coast.

munitions, supplies, troop trains or food supplies for the home population. From his office in Victoria Street, Walker ran the whole network: it and he could rely on the extraordinary dedication and care of the signalmen across the UK.

'Geddesburg': Monthouis, France

At the end of 1916 the weight of traffic caused a major crisis, with a breakdown of the rail system in northern France and the only occasion where there was a pile-up at the ports on both sides of the Channel. Again, a railwayman was brought in to sort things out, the most prominent manager and fixer of the whole war – Sir Eric Geddes, formerly General Manager of the North Eastern Railway and then troubleshooter for the Ministry of Munitions. He settled in the town of Monthouis – familiarly known as Geddesburg – and within two months had sorted out both the bottlenecks and an investment plan for new rail and light railways. The appointment of a civilian to a post formerly held by generals was strongly backed by Haig. Geddes organised double tracking – which had been little used on the single-track railways of northern France, apart from the main lines into Paris – and also reorganised the ports. The 1917 rail crisis was resolved and Geddes was then transferred to reorganise the Admiralty. He became the only non-royal in British history to be both an (honorary) major general and rear admiral.

Shirehampton/Swaythling/Southport/ Park Royal

Another logistical challenge was the largest effort ever organised for international transport of horses and mules. During the war period, 467,973 horses were purchased in the UK and 411,206 and 206,729 mules imported from the US and Canada respectively – plus a few thousand from Argentina. These had to be shipped and landed at Avonmouth and then taken by train to the remount depots. The veterinary services were very proud of their record in animal health: by 1918, out of 176 ships that carried animals from Canada and America to England, 76 completed the voyage without losing a single animal.[6]

Southampton, Hampshire

The BEF crossed in August 1914 from the docks at Southampton. This remained an important port both for cargo and for personnel going out to the Western Front:

> It was the Number 1 port [...] The largest shipment of troops in one day was on 22 August 1914: the largest shipment of horses in a week was in 1917 when just over ten thousand five hundred were shipped across. The largest amount of ammunition was in April 1917 [...] At noon on 24 November 1916 the ten thousandth special troop train entered the docks.

From June 1917 the port was extremely active with the transit of American troops:

> Practically every American soldier who went to France passed though Southampton and great numbers remained for some time in the American rest camp there. Everywhere they went they made friends, but in Southampton they were peculiarly at home.[7]

All roads lead to Southampton.

Newhaven, Sussex

The whole port area of Newhaven became a restricted zone for traffic in munitions and the female workforce employed to sort out shell cases came in daily by special trains from Brighton. It became an important port for the transport of munitions out and of salvage in.

Folkestone, Kent

East Kent had a ringside seat in the Great War, with events nearly every week by land, sea or air. Folkestone itself had more bombing raids than any other town and witnessed sea battles in the war against U-boats and destroyer raids. It was also the centre for intelligence networks in occupied France and Belgium, run from an office at 8 The Parade.

Folkestone was a town divided. There were the large nineteenth-century white villas on the cliff top, the most ambitious building programme on the south coast since Brighton under the Regency. The new villas were arranged in crescents and avenues going back from the Leas. At the front were the two largest hotels, the Metropole and the Grand. The servant class would have been on the top floors of the villas and tradesmen an occasional presence on the steps.

The old town, on the otherhand, was a different world of winding streets running down to the cramped harbour with its fishing and packet boats. Troops embarking would have seen the villas on the cliff top, but on disembarking the trains at Shorncliffe Station, now Folkestone West, and marching along the Leas, they would largely have bypassed the old town. The old alleyways, however, would have come into their own during leave or the frequent delays for bad weather or U-boat alarms.

In 1918 the Leas became an observation post for people who wanted to see the flash of gunfire or German bombs dropping on the base areas. For the 1918 raid on the hospitals in Etaples, the 'vibration was so great ... that Folkestone shook during its progress as the noise of the guns seemed only a few miles away'.[8] This followed the destroyer raid at about 1 a.m. on the night of 14 February 1918, with firing only a mile off the harbour: 'The thunder of the guns broke the stillness of the night and the streets of Folkestone re-echoed with the heavy reverberations.'[9] There was heavy loss of life when bombs fell on Tontine Street during evening shopping on Friday 25 May 1917. For Americans in transit in 1918 the 'echo of the guns across the Channel' was the first real sign of the war.

Folkestone, Shorncliffe (now Folkestone West station) where troops formed to march to the port.

The population of Folkestone grew from 30,000 to 100,000 during the war. Folkestone was the most open town on the coast. Many residents left the town and the large houses along Sandgate Road and Marine Parade were used as temporary rest camps for soldiers in transit. There must have been a strain on the local infrastructure (roads, water and electricity), as well as many opportunities for commerce and entertainment. Kent market gardening would have had a good time, but the fishermen could only watch in frustration the rising demand and soaring prices, as the war made fishing impossible off the Channel coast.

Folkestone came to be a very crowded town, where every yard of space in a restricted area between the hills and the sea was occupied by men in khaki. Night after night, the Pleasure Garden Theatre 'presented the appearance of a solid hard packed mass of khaki and similar conditions obtained in the cinemas'.[10] For locals there was the added excitement of seeing the famous prime ministers, generals and, in December 1918, President Woodrow Wilson (the first step taken by a US president-in-office in the UK was onto the quay at Folkestone) as they passed though. For some the visions were an anti-climax. As one soldier said after shaking Prime Minister Lloyd George's hand outside the Pavilion Hotel: 'I thought a wonderful lot of him but he's only like one of us.'[11]

The great majority of remaining permanent residents were women, as men joined the army. As John C. Carlile put it: 'Girls who had never been out before knew what it was to draw a wage that had been well

The Road of Remembrance in Folkestone. Most troops going to the Western Front marched down here.

Embarkation at Folkestone after the march.

and truly earned and life opened to them a new perspective.'[12] Folke-stone was possibly the most international town in the UK during the war period. Early in the war it gave shelter to 70,000 Belgians, but the Canadian presence was the most permanent, with all new recruits being trained here. Not all their activities were tolerated. In 1916 the first legislation banning the use of narcotics was passed as a result of Canadian soldiers 'riding the reindeer' after buying cocaine in Folkestone. Generally, however, relations with the Canadians were good. According to the Folkestone history the Canadian influence changed the local language so that 'You forgot to say yes because "Sure" was much more fashionable';[13] and the Canadian presence led to 'many a happy romance which ended in rice and confetti in Folkestone churches'.[14]

Dover, Kent

This was a restricted area with special passes required for entry. It was the base for the destroyers and drifters of the Dover patrol. The port was also used for soldiers returning as casualties and for ammunition ships.[15]

Richborough, Kent

This was a new port developed near Sandwich at one of the few points along the coast where it was possible to extend railway lines directly to deep water.[16] This was built for train ferries so that heavy guns, tanks and equipment could be carried directly to France. It was first used for cross-Channel barge traffic and then from 1917 for train ferries, after the example of those in Argentina (then owned by a British company) across the River Plate. The ferry landings were difficult to build because of the need to accommodate a 15ft tidal change. By 1917 most guns and heavy equipment were being shipped through Richborough, and for transport of munitions Richborough was second only to Newhaven in Sussex. An analysis made at the time found that 1,500 men were required for 1,000 tons of material using conventional methods and needing multiple unloading from factory to destination, while only 106 men were involved for the same amount of material transported by train ferry.

The tanks that provided Ludendorff with his 'black day' of the German Army were shipped through Richborough. On one day in September 1918 the British Army fired off a million shells, again transported through Richborough.

Richborough port in Kent – the mystery port – where the first train ferry in the UK departed from, an idea that came from Argentina.

By 1918 Richborough, the 'mystery port', had become a new town of huts where 20,000 were resident and many more came to work on a daily basis. The site contained over 500 buildings together with wharves, sidings, camps, warehouses, stores and shipyards. All has now disappeared, as have their successors in Pfizer's research labs.

Liverpool, Lancashire

With the U-boat offensives this came to be the vital port with the shortest sea crossing of the Atlantic. Its only rival was Clydeside. Liverpool had the great advantage that its piers were close to deep water in the Irish Sea. The high quality of its docks, which had been greatly extended just before the war, made for rapid docking and unloading. Liverpool was also close to consumers and munitions plants in the Midlands, which helped minimise wastage and storage problems.

Calais, France

Sixty thousand British personnel were based in the British area of Calais, including 2,000 women workers. Calais was a vast supply area, with reserves for 2 million men for two months, including a large

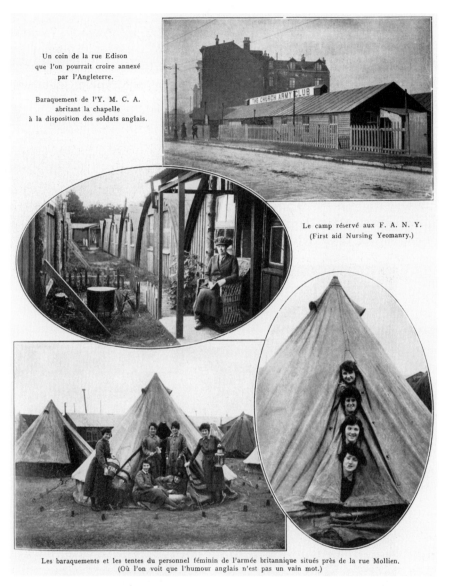

Un coin de la rue Edison
que l'on pourrait croire annexé
par l'Angleterre.

Baraquement de l'Y. M. C. A.
abritant la chapelle
à la disposition des soldats anglais.

Le camp réservé aux F. A. N. Y.
(First aid Nursing Yeomanry.)

Les baraquements et les tentes du personnel féminin de l'armée britannique situés près de la rue Mollien.
(Où l'on voit que l'humour anglais n'est pas un vain mot.)

Calais: 'annexé par l'Angleterre?'

depot for poison gas. Relations with local citizens were good, apart from the 'Scottish' riot of July 1918, in which seven gendarmes were killed.[17] However, as one area of Calais was British and another Belgian, German newspapers tried to drive a wedge between the Allies with stories that the British intended to keep Calais after the war. But the main local complaint was that the Royal Navy was not adequately protecting Calais. In 1918 came air attacks.

There was no civilian traffic through Calais, although there must have been some informal transit for weekend visits, with five or six ships sailing a day. There was a continued British presence well into 1919, with responsibility for sales of surplus equipment, including 250,000 beds.

Wimbledon, London

This was the site of a large railway yard where many of the Southern Railway trains were cleaned. It was a pioneering employer of women and the first place where women workers wore overalls. As mentioned earlier, these overalls were the precursor of the trouser suit.[18]

The first trouser suits.

Basingstoke, Hampshire

This was the site for the production of Thornycroft vehicles including the J Type lorry, of which 5,000 were built during the war. Thornycroft had originally been builders of boats, including the first torpedo boats, in Chiswick, and moved to Basingstoke to found a new company to make vehicles in 1898. The lorries were first used in the South African War and Thornycroft were pronounced the most reliable by Lord Kitchener in 1903.

There is an excellent display at the Milestones Museum, just outside Basingstoke, which includes a lorry from the First World War – registration NB 6684. This is a truck with an unladen weight of 2.75 tons and a carrying capacity of 4 tons. The vehicle is 7ft high and there is 4ft drop from the tailboard. There is a canvas hood that gives the driver protection from the weather. The driver was expected to do a great deal of maintenance and routine checks including adjustment of the gearbox and checking of oil. The tyres were solid on early models, which must have reduced changes but also made for discomfort and broken springs. The weight of the vehicle would have required a lot of muscle in the event of breakdown and the height of the tailboard must have made loading hard work: however, the truck was a lifesaver in bringing up supplies and carrying troops fast through danger areas.

From 1916 onwards British and Dominion troops benefited greatly from truck travel – now using pneumatic tyres. They could travel faster through the danger zone than could soldiers marching or in horse-drawn transport, and it was more difficult to hit a moving target. The use of trucks also made for more reliable supplies. Churchill recorded

Trucks like those made by vehicle manufacturer Thornycroft.

in 1918, on a visit near the front line, that he saw soldiers carried in a huge truck. It bounced on at speed, even though shells were falling around it.

Not all was left to the conscience of the truck driver. As C.S. Forester recorded in his novel *The General*:

> It became noticeable that in the Forty-fourth Corps area there were fewer lorries ditched while taking up supplies to the line at night. A ditched lorry meant that the driver was saved for that night from undergoing personal danger, whatever privations were caused to the men in the line. Curzon knew nothing of lorry driving, but saw to it that a driver who was ditched suffered so severely that no-one else was encouraged to follow his example. Motor-transport drivers remained influenced by the fear of a sentence of imprisonment to an extent far greater than in the infantry (the time was at hand when plenty of infantrymen would have welcomed a sentence of imprisonment which took them out of the line) and their savage sentences which Curzon obtained for delinquents made the chicken-hearted use their headlights at the risk of drawing fire, and to go on across dangerous crossroads however easily they could have staged a breakdown.[19]

At home, the war brought much more intensive use of roads within towns, as a vastly increased number of trucks were used for local traffic. Motoring had been a rich man's hobby, but with the war came the working-class driver and the woman driver and with the blackout roads became more dangerous. Traffic lights or stop signs were rare. Initially, the war brought a sudden reduction in numbers of horses because many were taken for use in France and later because of the greater availability of motorised transport.

The Thornycroft site is now a Morrisons supermarket. The only legacy of the factory is a crane marked 'Ransome and Rapier Ipswich load 10 tons' with a hook underneath the gantry. This stands over the entrance sign of Morrisons.

The Royal Navy

The Royal Navy had its own system of trains and routes; it was a separate world from the rest of the war effort. There were 'Jellicoe Specials' bringing coal from South Wales to the Grand Fleet in Scapa Flow, as well as a nightly train from Euston to Thurso. In addition there were trains from the Royal Navy cordite factory in Holton Heath, Dorset,

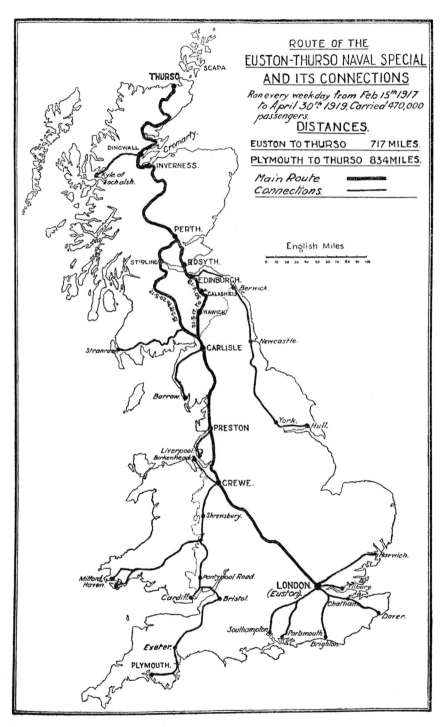

ROUTE OF THE
EUSTON-THURSO NAVAL SPECIAL
AND ITS CONNECTIONS
*Ran every week-day from Feb 15th 1917
to April 30th 1919. Carried 470,000
passengers.*
DISTANCES.
EUSTON TO THURSO   717 MILES.
PLYMOUTH TO THURSO   834 MILES.

Main Route
Connections.

English Miles

The route of the Naval Special.

to Scapa Flow. The long distances involved put a strain on rolling stock and on railwaymen. The Highland Railway was particularly stretched: it had been constructed as a single-track connection to a remote area.

Notes

1 Behrend, A., *The View from Kemmel Hill*, 1963, p. 11.
2 Pratt, E.A., *British Railways and the Great War*, Selwyn and Blount, 1921, p. 1,008.
3 Grieves, K., *Sir Eric Geddes*, Manchester University Press, 1989, pp. 30–1.
4 Hamilton, J.A.B. *Britain's Railways in World War 1*, Allen and Unwin, 1967, p. 36.
5 Northover, K., *Banbury During the Great War*, Prospero Publications, 2003, pp. 27–32.
6 SMEBE, p. 865.
7 Chapman-Huston, D. and Rutter, O., *General Sir John Cowans*, Hutchinson, 1924, pp. 217–18.
8 Carlile, J.C. (ed.), *Folkestone During the War,* F.J. Parsons, n.d.
9 Ibid.
10 Ibid, p. 216.
11 Ibid, p. 85.
12 Ibid, p. 205.
13 Ibid, p. 204.
14 Carlile, op cit.
15 George, M. and C., *Dover and Folkestone During the Great War*, Pen and Sword, 2008.
16 Butler, R., *Richborough Port*, Ramsgate Maritime Museum, n.d.
17 Chatelle, A., *Calais Pendant La Guerre 1914–18*, Librairie Aristide Quillet, Paris, 1927.
18 Pratt, op cit., p. 476.
19 Forester, C.S., *The General*, Penguin, 1956, p. 186.

5

New Weapons

It was in weapons development and improvement that the work of the managers paid off most. The German war effort had a few innovative managers such as Dr Fritz Haber, who developed gas warfare, and the military veteran Georg Bruchmüller, who introduced new techniques for artillery, but it was rare for the German military hierarchy to allow the kind of freedom enjoyed by the British innovators.

The developments took place at different sites throughout the Ministry's munitions empire. East Anglia and Lincolnshire were the key areas and the developments were in smaller firms that took initiatives which later won the support of the Ministry, usually as a result of intensive lobbying. The new weapon that was developed under the greatest central control – and with the most urgent priority – was also the biggest failure. Mustard gas, which was only produced a year after its first use by the enemy, had a casualty rate reported at one stage of 100 per cent among the workers making the gas and maintaining the equipment.

More important than new disruptive technology such as the tank were changes in technological sustainability, improving the value of well-established weapons. Thus the Survey Battalions greatly increased the impact of artillery both by increasing accuracy of fire and reducing the ability of German batteries to return fire. Much attention has been given by Bruchmüller to a few set pieces, but much less to the effect of bombardment hour after hour, which comes through so strongly in Ernst Jünger's *The Storm of Steel*.[1] Attrition really worked for the artillery – the wearing down turned the overwhelming and powerful German artillery of 1915 into a shadow of its former self by 1918, on most days firing 10 per cent or less of the Allied effort. Particularly severe was the effect on German supply lines, where journeys were slow and loads horse-drawn as the blockade prevented production of trucks with rubber tyres.

The principle of the mortar had been known for centuries – short-range projection of a missile from a metal tube – but it took a middle-aged industrialist and engineer from Ipswich, Sir Wilfred Stokes of Ransome and Rapier, to develop the most effective mortar of the war: the Stokes mortar. The Stokes mortar turned out to be versatile in using either explosives or gas shells, and was reliable, with few premature explosions. It could be set up quickly and was simple to use. While in 1915 the British had to hold the line with a terrible inadequacy in weaponry for trench warfare, by 1916 they were starting to get ample supplies of the most effective weaponry of the war.

War production started as a commodity business – the making of shells. In the second phase it moved to production of a much wider range of complex equipment. It was here that the skills of the mechanical engineering industry, particularly in the east of England, came into play. Women workers were important once again in a range of skilled jobs in manufacturing aircraft. There has been recognition of the great munitions success but perhaps not so much of the great speed of the second phase with its challenge of complex integration. There were few complains about design and quality and British industry also supplied much equipment for the new American Allies.

Lincoln, Lincolnshire

The best known innovation was the tank. This concept of an armoured vehicle to cross trench lines was aired in Whitehall soon after the start of the war by Winston Churchill and Colonel Swinton, but the actual work in designing and developing the tank was by William Foster & Co. in Lincoln.[2] The design grew from Foster's experience of producing agricultural equipment for the heavy soil of the fens. The French tank programme produced light tanks, which failed in 1917. The British design was for a heavy tank – the 1917 Mark IV model weighed 28 tons. Sir William Tritton, the managing director of Foster's, contributed the key design feature of caterpillar tracks, which went all round the whole body of the tank. (The caterpillar track that was so vital to the success of the tank – not used on most French-designed tanks – was invented in Grantham but the patent was sold before 1914 to an American company, now Caterpillar.) The tank was designed in early 1915 in an upstairs room in the White Hart Hotel in Lincoln, opposite the cathedral, by Sir William Tritton and Major Wilson, and was

The original tank built and tested by Foster's in 141 days.

tested in Hatfield Park on 2 February 1916. Colonel Swinton remained its godfather in Whitehall, even after Winston Churchill had left office, supervising the trials at Hatfield and the visit of the VIPs, who included Lloyd George, Kitchener and Balfour. Out of this trial came an order for 1,000 tanks.

The site of William Foster engineering is some distance from the White Hart Hotel at the bottom of the hill near the River Welland. It was part of a cluster of mechanical engineering firms. Siemens has taken over one part of the site in Tritton Way. The actual Foster's site is now used for the storage of fertiliser.

Foster's was taken over in the 1930s by the larger firm of Ruston Bucyrus, at one time a world leader in the manufacture of bucket excavators. It only survives in Lincoln as a ghostly sign on a wall. Livens, of the Livens projector, was the managing director of Rushton during the war.

Tanks were tested some distance away to the west of Lincoln in Burton's Park, on another part of the ridge, which rises out of the flat Lincolnshire landscape.

Hatfield Park, Hertfordshire

This was the site selected by Colonel Swinton for the trial on 2 February 1915. He designed 'A steeplechase course' with the same dimensions as those of the latest German defences. This was an ideal place far from prying eyes for the trial of 'the new monster the machine gun eater.' The tank was brought by rail and unloaded at night and performed perfectly in trench crossing, both on 2 February and on the repeat performance for the King on 8 February.

Hatfield House, seat of the Cecil family (including the Victorian prime minister, the Marquis of Salisbury) can be visited April–October, and some of the ditches over the Swinton course can be seen in the grounds.

Oldbury, Staffordshire

In 1917 tank production shifted to a larger factory that had been used for assembling passenger trains. This was Metropolitan Carriage and Wagon – the Black Country had become host to larger plants, while Birmingham mainly specialised in workshop-based industries. There was also more space for a testing ground closer to the factory than was the case in Lincoln. Most of the Mark IV tanks were built there, though using designs from Foster's. By the time of the Armistice it was building the Mark V, which had a simpler driving system and a much improved Ricardo engine.

Elveden, Norfolk

This was an estate of the Guinness family near Thetford. Tanks were brought down by train from Lincoln for testing. The 'Heavy Section Machine Gun Corps' would eventually move from Bisley to Elveden Camp, where six companies of tanks were raised.

Bovington, Dorset

This was where the Tank Corps was developed from 1917 onwards and is now the site of the Tank Museum, which is well worth a visit. Tanks were unloaded at Wool station, where the loading ramps are still visible. The testing ground is much as it was in 1918 and still used for testing military vehicles.

The lead role then passed to France and the Heavy Section (of the Machine Gun Corps), later renamed the Tank Corps. It was the inspired leadership of General Elles and his team, notably Colonel Fuller, which turned the tank into a successful weapon. Many helped to develop the tank, but it was one man, the military thinker Fuller, who developed the Tank Corps as an arm in which the problems of logistics, maintenance, communication and crew health were addressed. He also attracted military innovators such as Baker-Carr, who commanded the first tank brigade. In 1917 the tank showed at the Battle of Cambrai that, in combination with new artillery tactics, it could bring about a breakthrough, even if only a temporary one. The attack was led by Elles himself and his eve of battle message was one from a man with a superb gift for leadership. He had originally asked Fuller to write it, but Fuller passed the pad back saying 'You do it':[3]

Special order No. 6
Tomorrow the Tank Corps will have the chance of which they have been waiting for many months—to operate on good going in the van of battle.

All that hard work and ingenuity can achieve has been done in the way of preparation.

It remains for Unit Commanders and tank crews to complete the work by judgement and pluck in the battle itself.

In the light of past experience, I leave the good name of the Corps with great confidence in your hands.

I propose leading the attack of the centre division.

Major General M.J. Elles CB DSO.
Commanding the Tank Corps in France.
Cambrai 19 November 1917.
Distribution: To Tank Commanders.
FEAR NAUGHT.

With it came an Elles-designed flag – brown, red and green – 'From mud through blood to the green fields beyond', a description originally attributed to Fuller and now the inscription on the Tank Corps memorial in Whitehall, behind the Old War Office.

In 1918 the Tank Corps had some great days, notably at the Battle of Amiens, when 400 tanks led an 8-mile penetration through the German lines. Maintenance and support problems weakened the tank presence but the new weapon continued to have an impact on the nerves of the German Army.

Ipswich, Suffolk

The Stokes mortar also came from East Anglia, a further addition to the remarkable wartime record of innovation by engineering companies in the East of England. As the Munitions Committee handbook for East Anglia summed it up: 'Of the forty-two Boards of management through the country East Anglia comes third upon the list for output, being only surpassed by London and Manchester.'[4] What had been seen as a remote area became central to the war with a massive expansion of the naval base at Harwich and the largest seaplane base off the shingle at Yarmouth.

The Stokes mortar, which was developed at Sir Wilfred Stokes' plant in Ipswich, was one of many examples of flexibility and quality production by manufacturers in East Anglia. They also made a vital contribution in 1918 to cope with a sudden shortage of aircraft radiators through the Motor Radiators manufacturing plant in Sudbury: 'The factories at Greet and Sudbury were of the greatest value for emergency work throughout 1918.'[5]

Civil engineer Sir Wilfred Stokes was managing director of Ransome and Rapier in Ipswich, which made railway equipment, including the giant buffers still visible at Waterloo Station in London. The mortar was manufactured in Ipswich and at other sites, including Woolwich. An associated company also in Ipswich actually had a more notable record of innovation, having produced the first commercially available powered lawnmower in 1902. It is not quite clear how Sir Wilfred (by this time aged 54) invented his mortar, but he seems to have benefited from it, receiving £1 royalties for each Stokes mortar bomb produced. Given there were 1,636 Stokes mortars on the Western Front, each capable of firing thirty bombs a minute, this must been quite a lucrative arrange-

Shell making at the Orwell plant in Ipswich, makers of the Stokes mortar.

ment. His nephew, Richard Stokes, took over from him as managing director (and as MP for Ipswich became the leading opponent in the Commons of strategic bombing in the Second World War). Sir Wilfred was working at the time for the innovation department of the Ministry of Munitions and it was Lloyd George's personal support that was crucial.

Cambridge, Cambridgeshire

The most important sustaining innovation was the Field Survey – a combination of methods for targeting guns and identifying the location of enemy guns. When the BEF went to war in 1914 there were two officers, two clerks and one printing company to keep the force supplied with maps. The army had to rely for the next year on French maps, which were out-of-date and inaccurate. By the end of the war there were five Field Survey battalions, one for each army, each 800–1,000 strong. A special workshop made thousands of maps a month. The Old Cavendish laboratory is in J.J. Thomson Avenue, formerly called Free School Lane, which is where Lawrence Bragg worked, along with his father, and where they won their joint Nobel Prize in 1915 for their work on the structure of crystals. The new Cavendish laboratory has been built on another site but the buildings of the old one are still there. Cambridge also supplied many of the instruments for sound-ranging through the Cambridge Scientific Instruments Company, based in the area, founded by Horace Darwin, who was working with Bragg in his sound-ranging team. The later Pye Group was founded by a foreman from this company, William G. Pye. They probably had contact with Marconi, manufacturer of radio equipment based in Chelmsford. Thus the advances in sound-ranging grew out of a network in East Anglia.

The Royal Engineers, who ran the field survey, developed new methods of identifying gun location. One was flash-spotting, which was most useful on flat ground at night. Another was sound-ranging, a more elaborate system requiring six microphones spaced out to monitor the sound waves. Sound-ranging was developed by Lawrence Bragg in a somewhat unusual way:

> The solution came in stages. First it was clear in a number of ways that although the gun report produced very little impression on the ear it was associated with large pressure changes. It rattled windows. In our billet at La Clytte of the usual Belgian farmhouse type, the privy was in an annexe opening out of the kitchen with no outer door

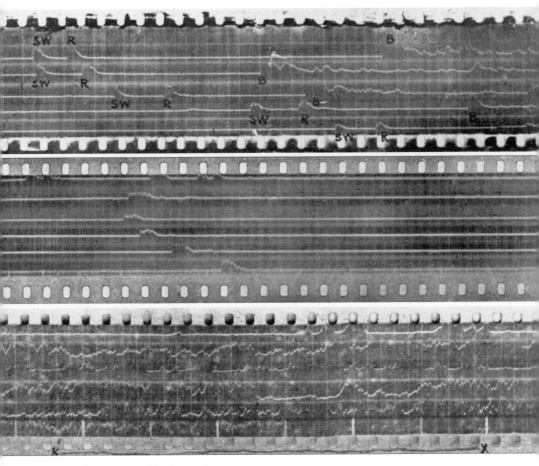

Sound-ranging and flash-spotting.

or window [...] The deafening shell wave of a six-inch gun which
fired over us left one's posture undisturbed, whereas the faint gun
report had a marked lifting effect.[6]

Corporal Tucker, formerly of the Imperial College physics department,
then showed how these waves could be recorded by using six special
microphones in a line – later named Tucker microphones. By 1917 the
British were intercepting an order showing just how effective Bragg's
'show' had become:

Group order
In consequence of the excellent sound-ranging of the English, I forbid
any battery to fire when the whole sector is quiet, especially in an
East wind. Should there be occasion to fire; the adjoining battery

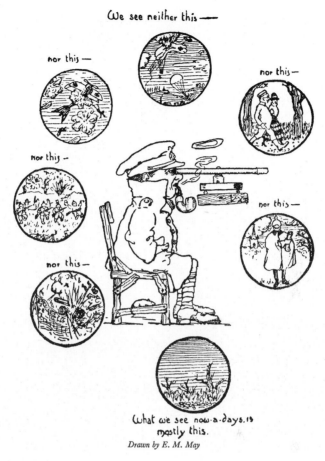

Drawn by E. M. May

The keys to victory in the War of the Guns.

must always be called upon, either directly or through the Group, to fire a few rounds.[7]

The new weapons were most effective when used together. The first full use of survey techniques was the tank-led Battle of Cambrai in November 1917 and was the first use of advance registration so that the bombardment could be followed by an attack within minutes: 'Surprise was to be the key to success.'

It was also by accident that the proper use of Field Survey battalions in preparing an attack was discovered. Although Cambrai was the first 'survey' battle, it was not made so deliberately. It became so because it was decided to prepare a tactical scheme that would give the tanks a chance to show what they could do. The whole scheme was prepared to suit the tanks.

Left: The Royal Artillery Memorial at Hyde Park Corner.

It was laid down that there were three prerequisites if the tanks were to be successful:

1) No Artillery registration.
2) No attempt to destroy obstacles by preliminary bombardment.
3) Artillery to be directed on guns instead of on trenches and wire.[8]

The decisions about the battlefield were increasingly coming to be made by technicians, not just by generals.

Porton Down, Wiltshire

The first new weapon was chemical warfare – the use of chlorine-based gas – and Porton Down became the most important site for research and development into gas, including the testing of gas masks. The experimental ground at Porton on Salisbury Plain was purchased in January 1916 and on this site complete laboratories were built and trenches and dugouts constructed for the conduct of field experiments. The site can be seen in the distance from the road south of the main plain but access is highly restricted, as it is still the main UK centre for chemical warfare research.

The Germans maintained the initiative throughout the war in chemical warfare and by 1918 half of the shells fired by German artillery were gas shells. As a later American review summed up: 'The phenomenal rise of chemicals from an unknown obscurity in 1915 to a position of a military agent of the first magnitude in 1918 is without parallel in the history of warfare.'[9]

The crisis after the first gas cloud in April 1915 north of Ypres was bad enough but would have been far worse had the German generals believed in their own weapon. The gas discharge from cylinders was released late in the afternoon without adequate reinforcements to follow it up and take advantage of the several-thousand-yard breach in the Allied line. The six corps that might have followed the gas cloud had been sent to fight the Russians. The Allied defence was also helped by the rapid dissipation of the gas. Unless highly concentrated the chlorine gas dissipates in the atmosphere quite quickly.

The German Army in fact made little use of chlorine and phosgene after the first gas cloud. It was a boomerang weapon, which favoured the Allies, as the prevailing wind was from the west. Until the coming of gas shells in 1916 there was no route by which the German Army could actually deliver much gas. It was only with the coming of mustard gas, 'The king of battlefield gases' and produced in great quantities by the powerful German chemical industry, that gas shells were widely used. Mustard gas may have prolonged the war by several months, as it did not dissipate but remained behind to contaminate the ground, making it difficult for men and impassable for animals. According to one German post-war evaluation:

> The German front would never have succeeded in withstanding the powerful onslaught and concentrated forces and war matériel of almost the whole world if German chemists had not at that moment held the protective shield of the Yellow Cross Substance (mustard gas) before the German soldiers.[10]

The weapon that started as the great war-winning innovation ended as a chemical fence.

The British research with gas had begun before the Ypres cloud, but only into tear gas, which was permitted under the Hague Convention. In December 1914 some officers who had served in France inquired about the possibility of using 'stink bombs' to clear dugouts. Chemists at Imperial College tried dozens of substances and chose Ethyl iodoacetate, partly because large supplies of bromine, from which it could be distilled, were available from South America.[11] The gas was called 'SK' after South Kensington where it was developed, and was first used by the British at Loos in September 1915.

The battlefield response was by a military entrepreneur, the dynamic Charles Foulkes. The main British response to Ypres was to form the Special Brigade.[12] The leader, Major Foulkes, had no previous connections with the chemical industry, but he was recommended by Robertson for the post, as it seemed to require great initiative. Robertson recalled that he had met such an individual ten years earlier in Sierra Leone. This young officer, during personal leave and entirely on his own initiative, had visited a fortress, sketched its fortifications, taken telescopic photographs and presented these to headquarters on his return.[13] Foulkes was an individual who thrived on combat and danger. He rejected descriptions of the Western Front as a 'nightmare of blood and horror' and preferred to face danger with 'a joke and a smile'.

The Special Brigade developed a new way of delivering the gas using the Livens projector, which uses a mortar to propel a gas bomb several hundred metres through the air. Livens was an engineer and company director from Ruston Bucyrus in Lincoln, yet another example of low-cost innovation emerging out of East Anglia. A row of Livens projectors could deliver an intense dose to a limited area; because of the short distance the shell case could be thin and could deliver 50 per cent gas content, compared to 12 per cent for an artillery gas shell. Such discharges were a dreaded surprise, since they did not leave troops time to put on their masks. As the account by Jünger in *The Storm of Steel* put it:

> The frequent attacks were unpleasant and claimed many victims. They were carried out by means of hundreds of iron cylinders buried in the earth and discharged by electricity in a salvo of flame. As soon as the light showed gas-alarm was given and anyone who has not his mask on and flap well tucked in found himself in a bad way. In many spots too the gas reached an absolute density, so that even the mask was useless since there was literally no oxygen to breathe. Consequently there were many casualties.[14]

A later American estimate was that the Special Brigade of 7,000 men inflicted 145,000 casualties on the German Army.[15]

Avonmouth, Gloucestershire

Less success was won by the British effort to produce mustard gas. There had been effective manufacture of phosgene at Greenford, while chlorine was traded from the French for a shell-filling plant in Calais; but the Allies went their separate ways on mustard gas with remarkably little co-ordination, as both hit major problems. In the British case there is a frank account in the Ministry of Munitions History on the problems at the chosen site near Avonmouth[16]:

> The peculiar difficulties involved in dealing with (mustard gas) gave rise to serious problems as to plant and ventilation, but, owing to the urgency of the demand attention was concentrated on output.

There was little improvement through 1918. At one time, 'the workers actually engaged on charging had nearly 100 per cent casualties while for a considerable period one casualty was reported for every six to nine shells that left the factory'.[17]

It was only in September 1918 that mustard gas was available, but if the war had continued into 1919 much more would have been available both from the UK and from a vast expansion in American production. The 'king of battlefield gases', thankfully, would have reigned over an empty battlefield.

There was some success in defensive measures, with the development of the small box respirator in which the troops had confidence. It was noted in the March 1918 offensive that if all other equipment was discarded the troops held on to their gas masks. German gas masks had to be made from leather, as the blockade had cut off supplies of rubber. By 1918 there was also the development of protective wear against mustard gas, which could lie on the ground for days and get into clothing. The situation would have been far worse if the Germans had the steel to make thicker shells with up to 50 per cent gas content rather than the 12 per cent that was the most common. Any shells from the Allies in 1919 would have been at least 50 per cent and the German Army would have had impossible problems in finding new clothing to replace contaminated uniforms. Perhaps the spectre of an army without uniforms contributed to Ludendorff's nervous collapse in August 1918 (a psychiatrist was consulted and recommended more rest and leisure).

From 1917 it was decided to build new plants to produce mustard gas. These were to be at Avonmouth and Chittening on the Severn estuary near Bristol. Manufacturing was at Avonmouth and the charging and filling of the shells was carried out 2 miles north at Chittening. Owing to the urgent demands of the service, practically all other considerations were sacrificed to output, with the result that the work was carried on under very bad conditions.

The Avonmouth site is now empty as a derelict chemical works. The Chittening site is close to a small resort at Severn Beach and is a mile from the current site of the second Severn crossing.

Imperial College, South Kensington

The early gas research was carried out at Imperial College, which had been developed close to the site of the Great Exhibition of 1851 in Hyde Park. The chosen substance was tested in the grounds of Imperial College, now a car park:

> Tests were made in a trench at Imperial College. Col (later General Sir Louis) Jackson came from the War Office to attend them. He was more resistant to tear gas than the academics (or maybe he shut his eyes tightly) but eventually he too succumbed. Further confirmation of the compound was provided by a lad who happened

A horse and man in gas masks.

to be passing by. So the substance was adopted and to commemorate South Kensington it was code named SK.[18]

The young lad was paid 1*s* for his part in the experiment.

Greenford, Middlesex

Most of the chlorine gas was produced in France using French methods. Greenford was developed to produce phosgene gas at a new plant on what was then agricultural land. However, the area had both a record and a future in chemicals, with the site of the first experiment in synthetic dyes by Perkin and Co. quite close, and the future Glaxo pharmaceutical plant next door. It is on the banks of the Grand Union Canal and close to the Great Western Railway. This site made all the phosgene gas needed for the rest of the war. The site is now occupied by an industrial estate.

Boots, Nottingham, Nottinghamshire

This was the initial site for making the first effective gas masks, the so-called large-box respirators. Some 200,000 of these were produced for use by machine-gunners and artillery personnel. The gas was filtered through granules. The Boots building is still there.

Later there was a demand for a lighter version and the chemist Edward Harrison, who provided 'both research and organisational genius', developed the small-box respirator, which could be used by the infantry as well: 'Every soldier was individually fitted with his mask and then exposed to tear gas in a chamber for five minutes.'[19]

Holloway, London

Boots continued to make masks but to meet the need for much greater numbers they were also made at Batavia Mills in Holloway. Special masks were made for horses, mules and dogs; however, it was not possible to protect animals against contact with ground contaminated with mustard gas.

Notes

1 Jünger, E., *The Storm of Steel*, Chatto and Windus, 1929, pp. 92–3
2 William Foster and Co., *The Tank, Its Birth and Development*, Wellington Foundry, Lincoln, 1919.
3 Fuller, J.F.C., *Memoirs of an Unconventional Soldier*, pp. 200–1.
4 East Anglia Munitions Comm Stokes W., *A Short History of the East Anglian Munitions Committee in the Great War 1914–18*, n.d.
5 *Official History of the Ministry of Munitions*, Vol. VIII, Control of Industrial capacity and Equipment, 1922, Naval and Military Press, p. 212.
6 Bragg, L., 'Sound-Ranging', in Bragg, L. et al, *Artillery Survey in the First World War 1914–18*, Field Survey Association, 1971.
7 Ibid.
8 Innes, J.R., *Flash Spotters and Sound Rangers*, George Allen and Unwin, 1935, p. 25.
9 Prentiss, A., *Chemicals in War*, McGraw-Hill, 1937, p. 684.
10 Haber, L.F., *The Poisonous Cloud*, OUP 1986.
11 Haber, op. cit.
12 Foulkes, C.H., *Gas: The Story of the Special Brigade*, Blackwood, 1934, p. 272.
13 Richter, D., *Chemical Soldiers*, Leo Cooper, 1994.
14 Jünger, op. cit., p. 238.
15 Prentiss, op. cit.
16 *Official History of the Ministry of Munitions*, Vol. VIII, Control of Industrial Capacity and Equipment, 1922, Naval and Military Press/IWM, pp. 181–3.
17 *Official History*, op. cit., p. 173.
18 Haber, p. 51.
19 Jones, S., *World War I Gas Warfare Tactics and Equipment*, Osprey, 2007.

6

The War at Sea

Not many men realised that for some time past the average life of a
ship had been about ten round voyages.[1]

This war at sea has received far less attention than the war on the Western Front but involved almost as many people: 1.4 million, including
the Royal Navy, merchant seamen, fishermen and dock workers. The
axis of the war shifted with conflict first in the North Sea and then, in
1917, a move to the Atlantic approaches. It was a war that drew on
seagoing skills developed around the British Isles rather than just on
training provided by the authorities. As one of the official historians
put it:

> The British Navy was at its appointed stations; the temper of a
> seafaring people, self-reliant, resourceful and indomitable, was
> everywhere, and shone like a phosphorescence over thousands of
> unregarded acts of sacrifice.[2]

The action at sea began on the first day of the war, and the following
months were a time of menace. From 1904 to 1914 the navy had begun
to adapt to a revolution in weapons with the coming of the Dreadnought, the submarine, the torpedo and the sea mine. In addition there
was wireless telegraphy, the seaplane and new firing systems involving
synchronised firing controlled from the upper mast. The 'Fisher revolution', named after Admiral Lord Fisher, had also involved changes in
naval personnel, with more intensive training, especially in engineering.

In addition, there had to be new bases, as the old bases faced an
enemy to the west. The North Sea was a British lake. Now the North

The loss of a British merchant ship. The average life of a ship would have been about ten round voyages.

Sea was under threat. The new weapons also meant that the old strategy of the close blockade was no longer feasible, especially as the German bases were highly protected both by estuaries and by minefields. The deterrent weapon of the Grand Fleet had to be based at Scapa Flow in the Orkneys. Harwich and Dover were the forward bases for protecting the Channel crossing and merchant shipping passing through the Downs off East Kent.

The first weeks showed that the mine and the submarine were powerful and deadly weapons. German ships – including the liner *Empress of Berlin* – were active in mine laying. One submarine, U19, torpedoed three older cruisers, *Aboukir*, *Cressy*, and *Hogue*, off the Belgian coast on 22 September with the loss of 1,359 lives. The battleship *Audacious* was sunk by a mine on 27 September in the Irish Sea. To all this had to be added the naval disaster off Chile, at the Battle of Coronel, and the bombardment of Scarborough, Hartlepool and Whitby. The first phase of the war at sea went very badly, threatening the reputation of the young First Lord of the Admiralty, Winston Churchill.

In the Atlantic approaches the submarine U21 was to sink the *Lusitania* on 7 May 1915, an action that led to eighteen months of retreat from the most intensive form of the submarine campaign, but German interest in the new weapon remained strong. Before the sinking of the three old cruisers there had been little interest in submarines and no clear plan for future development. However, a torpedo that blew a hole under the water line with a small explosive charge, causing the force of water pressure to sink a large ship in few minutes was impressive and tempting to warlords with a deficit in war-winning weapons.

Even so, in the first phase of the war the submarine in fact achieved little. Of the 100 British ships sunk between August and December 1914, 42 were sunk by mines, 55 by raiders and only 3 by submarines.

There was a series of very dire events crammed into a few weeks. The bombardment of Scarborough, Hartlepool and Whitby on 16 December 1914 was the first attack on the English coast since John Paul Jones had fired on Whitehaven in Cumbria during the American War of Independence. The loss of life inflicted by mines and torpedoes struck whole streets in naval towns such as Portsmouth, where the families of crewmen lived close together. And then came the sinking of the *Lusitania*. But there was success in protecting merchant shipping and in the Battle of the Dogger Bank the British cruisers were victorious. By mid-1915 it was not quite sea business as usual but some fishing had restarted, the blockade of Germany was in place and the Grand Fleet was safe in Scapa Flow behind nets.

The war in the North Sea became routine, with frequent interception of merchant ships in the Channel at the Downs – the stretch of sheltered water between the Goodwin Sands and the Kent coast, where ships were stopped and searched. In the course of the war some 80,000 ships were stopped and searched in the Downs. There was also a cordon in the north between Iceland and Scotland, where the 10th Cruiser Squadron – in fact mainly made up of passenger ships – intercepted ships heading for Scandinavia. There were set channels off the East Coast to be kept clear of mines.

In 1916 came the surprise sortie of the German High Seas Fleet, leading to the Battle of Jutland. The German Fleet only spent twenty hours outside its harbour, putting little pressure on the meagre living accommodation in ships designed to leave space for heavy armour plating. At Jutland the Germans sank more ships than the British but achieved no lasting strategic success.

Jutland led to rethinking by the German leadership. Enthusiasm for submarines had grown during the period of restrictions, as had the building programme for long-range submarines. In February 1917 unrestricted submarine warfare – sinking on sight – was declared. For the war at sea this shifted the main arena from the North Sea to the Atlantic Approaches.

At first the new policy seemed to be working, with many thousands of tons of shipping sunk. There were 2,500 arrivals at British ports each week but many of these were coasters or smaller steamers from Europe. The key manager of Allied shipping, Sir Arthur Salter, wrote:

The arrival of British ocean going ships comparable to the forty lost was not 2,500 but 140 (a week). At the peak of submarine success 25 per cent of ships sailing were being sunk before returning to their home port.[3]

The Admiralty advised that it might not be possible to continue the war into 1918 and John Jellicoe, now First Sea Lord, called for a land offensive in Flanders for 1917 to close its submarine bases. However, the coming of the convoy made a vast difference, suddenly the sea was empty. It turned out to be as difficult to spot twenty ships as to spot one.[4] The convoys were heavily protected by airships and seaplanes as well as by naval vessels and from the summer of 1917 they also had protection from an increasing number of American destroyers. Convoys were difficult for lone U-boats to attack.

This Atlantic phase of the war at sea was the war of the destroyers. They had the speed and endurance to escort convoys and they could use the new weapon of the depth charge. The trawlers continued to have the main role in inshore waters off Cornwall and into the Channel and they were assisted by fast motorboats made in the US. Liverpool came to be even more important, as a port with a short sea route around the north of Ireland.

The Atlantic phase was also a severe test of the endurance of merchant seamen, but losses were greatly reduced as the convoys speeded up and larger liners were used to transport troops. However, little could improve the atrocious weather in the North Atlantic and the Bay of Biscay. In peacetime, shipping traffic was reduced in winter (the Blue Riband winners of the Hamburg Amerika line could not take the North Atlantic in winter and Chief Executive Albert Ballin had to invent the Mediterranean cruise to make use of the ships). The passengers stayed away and goods were stored, but increased wartime traffic meant that ports and storage areas had to be cleared quickly. Merchant shipping became a year-round activity and one that was highly efficiently organised, helped by rapid transit through the docks and on the railways.

The main initiative in the Channel was to set up an improved barrage to block the straits. This was finally achieved in early 1918 with a line of drifters from Folkestone to Cap Gris Nez in France,[5] which was lighted at night to a pattern advised by the fireworks expert Wing Commander Brock, focing submarines to go round the north of Scotland. Attempts were then made to lay a continuous line of mines from Inverness to Norway – a line finished shortly before the Armistice. The British were not enthusiastic about this scheme, which was an

The convoy system.

American creation, but, not for the last time, the crucial argument was that the Americans were paying the bill.

The navy had its special logistics and supply lines and would not share facilities with the army or collaborate with the Ministry of Munitions and this even extended to the post-war history, as the Admiralty did not agree with the official history of the Ministry of Munitions. The special cordite plant was at Holton Heath in Dorset, although there were problems with the stability of the cordite, which probably contributed to several explosions. There were special trains from South Wales to Inverness carrying coal and a daily 'Jellicoe Special' from Euston to Thurso for naval personnel, who would then proceed on by ferry to Scapa Flow. The navy started the war with its own air service and this developed faster than the Royal Flying Corps, experimenting with long-range bombing raids. Intensive use was made of seaplanes. Most of the navy's aircraft were, however, transferred to the new RAF in April 1918.

Thus the war at sea started with '22 months of setback' and ended with success.[6] The blockade denied Germany food and vital war materials such as rubber. The High Seas Fleet was interned at Scapa Flow. Yet the results were only achieved with great controversy, which coloured the entire management of the war at sea. By the end of 1917 the politicians had installed their own nominees in top positions, including Sir Eric Geddes as First Lord of the Admiralty. The brass hats at the War Office managed to fight off the politicians more effectively than did the proud admirals across Whitehall. The sea war, then, finally presented a picture of great success – but won through times of great anxiety.

New technology included the depth charge, the geophone for acoustic detection of submarines, and the paravane for clearing mines. The navy had its own research establishment with Professor Bragg, father of Lawrence Bragg of sound-ranging, as a leader. The development of the Naval Auxiliary Force of trawlers in the first six months of the war was a critical step, without which access to British ports might have been blocked.

The untiring blockade and the defeat of German naval power were crucial to success. The Imperial German Navy seemed to have an inferiority complex summed up by the passivity of its forces in the Channel and its failure to repeat the early raids on the coast with any frequency. The German Navy was compelled to avoid losses in ships, due to orders coming directly from the Kaiser.

The war at sea also depended on the seamanship of those in the Merchant Navy. Convoys required strict discipline, as did the unloading of goods at crowded ports. Notable, too, was the contribution of the dockers, as the number and weight of cargoes increased.

Grimsby, Lincolnshire

To meet the new threats, the navy had to expand the Naval Auxiliary Force using the fishing fleet as well as volunteer paddle steamers and yachtsmen. This started with the largest fishing boats – the trawlers. Minesweeping experiments had been tried with both destroyers and tugs but these did not work. In 1907 the commander of the Channel Fleet, Admiral Lord Charles Beresford, visited Grimsby and inspected some trawlers:

> Here were the men accustomed to deal with trawl ropes and trawls, the equivalent to mine sweeps. These fishermen were so expert at their work that they never fouled the screws with the wire ropes and their ships were fitted with steam winches and all the necessary gear required for sweeping.[7]

Trials of sweeping by trawlers were successful. At the start of the war over 200 trawlers were recruited into the Auxiliary Force, many based at Dover and Harwich. They turned out to be highly effective – but at a cost in casualties. The German mines were powerful and sensitive and any contact between the steel hull of the trawler and the horns of the mine brought disaster. One trawler was blown up for every 200 mines cleared. The trawler crews paid for the failure to develop purpose-built minesweepers.

Steam trawlers minesweeping in a pair with a wire between them, an improvised and highly dangerous activity.

Some dynamism in port: Scotch fisher girls barreling herrings.

The trawler crews had to move to different areas at the start of the war depending on where German mines were located, but later their sweeping duties took on a pattern. They swept key channels, including a 10-mile channel up the East Coast, and this was done twice a day for the main routes. German mine-laying became a frequent, almost daily, occurrence and the crews started using mine-laying submarines that could lay fifteen mines without surfacing. In general, the trawler efforts were a success in defeating what had seemed likely to be a major menace, and they continued in this role throughout the war. They were welcomed by the navy – trawler crews were now allowed to use the canteens on battleships, which had not been the case before 1914.

There were also British efforts at laying minefields, hampered by the lack of mine-layers and the poor quality of British mines. There were heavy casualties when the old battleship HMS *Bulwark* blew up in Sheerness in 1915 while being loaded with mines. This was blamed on inexperienced workers.

Scapa Flow, The Orkneys

This was by far the largest base and the one with the greatest logistical support, with special coal trains and the nightly special from Euston.[8] It also had the greatest number of admirals, led by the commander of the Grand Fleet, first John Jellicoe then David Beatty. Even in Trafalgar Square, Jellicoe, 'the only man who could lose the war in an afternoon', has a slightly worried look and his picture in his memoir is self-effacing. Beatty, on the other hand, became the most famous fighting Admiral since Nelson and his bust even adorns the approach to Union Station in Kansas City.

In 1910 the *Aberdeen Free Press* had written of the Pentland Firth, the 10-mile strait between the Scottish mainland and the Orkneys: 'there is more potency for evil to a pint in that bit of water than any other stretch of water in the wide world.'[9] Coming out of the calm flow, ships could then be caught by a 10-knot tide. As Jellicoe wrote:

A ship emerging from the slack water into the full strength of the tide could be, and sometimes was, caught on the bow by the force of the fast moving water to be swung round through 90 or even 180 degrees so that she was heading back the way she had come, an extreme danger to all following vessels as she could be nearly unmanageable. Such a situation on a dark night with a large fleet showing no lights

Scapa Flow – view looking South from Houton Bay.

was not pleasant and it speaks well for the skill shown in handling
the ships that no accident occurred from this cause.[10]

A signal 'prepare to leave Scapa' was made and all ships raised steam
for 18 knots at two hours notice – steam-driven vessels did not have
starter motors like cars. A second signal would then give sailing distances and routes. Provision was also made for squadrons to pass
alternately north and south of the Pentland Skerries (rocky islets of
extreme menace) when going east into the North Sea.

Most of the time the Grand Fleet was anchored in the Flow, while the
destroyers went out on patrol after submarines or mine-layers. There
were days of drama, such as the Battle of Jutland on 31 May–1 June 1916
and the loss of the *Hampshire*, with Lord Kitchener on board, when it
struck a mine on the evening of 5 June during a severe summer gale.

There were 100,000 personnel at Scapa and efforts were made to
provide them with recreation. There was sport, vegetable allotments,
and even a 9-hole golf course together with evening entertainments.
German admirals after the war expressed envy of these activities, which
were not available in Wilhelmshaven, where it was felt that extreme
boredom had contributed to the final mutinies in 1918.

The presence of the fleet led to a vast increase in local supply business for meat, bread and clothing. The farmers were involved and the

The USS *New York* arrives at Scapa.

money made enabled tenants to buy their own farms. A local tailor, Peter Shearer, designed a special overcoat for the Services, which became famous as the 'British Warm'. It was more informal than the full dress outfit and made of softer, warmer material. There was even a branch of the Army and Navy Stores at Kirkwall. The capital of the Orkneys was not large but had an unusual number of public houses. The spirit of abstinence contended with the spirit of commerce in the native land of whisky. However, there were also frustrations as well as earnings for the local population, with permits required and the islands in effect under martial law administered by (retired) naval dugouts.

At the end Scapa was the scene of drama with the arrival of the German fleet for internment on 23–24 November 1918, and then the scuttling of the ships by their crews on 21 June 1919 (all flying German ensigns 'of the largest possible size'), in protest against the peace terms of the Versailles Treaty. Scapa Flow then had to readjust to peacetime, as the population of 25,000 Orcadians took up their daily routines with occasional visits from salvage parties for the German ships.

Harwich, Essex

'The dominant note was always the siren.'[11] The destroyers were based at Parkeston Quay on the River Stour, which 'saw action' on most days

Cartoon of the Harwich Commander, 'the Tyrwhitt Tyr-woo'. He was an outstanding local commander.

up to 1916. The battle was sometimes only a few miles away and could include German submarines, mine-layers or destroyers. Admiral Tyrwhitt was the most junior officer to receive a parliamentary grant (of £10,000) and on becoming a baronet took his title from the Dutch light vessel that had been in daily use as a reference point, *Tyrwhitt of Terschelling*.

It was off Harwich on 5–6 August 1914 that both the British and the Germans had their first vessels sunk – the mine-layer *Konigin Luise* for Germany and the cruiser *Amphion* for Britain, which was sunk by one of the mines laid. 'The War just behind the tennis court' continued with Harwich getting visits first from surface mine-layers and then from mine-laying submarines. Tyrwhitt, like Keyes and Beatty, became famous, as well as popular and well respected. A photograph of Tyrwhitt was turned into a patriotic postcard – much to his disgust:

The pattern of the recall signal was that each cruiser in the harbour taking her time from the flagship sounded both her sirens thrice, each blast being three minutes long. To supplement the signal the Alexandra Hotel, where there were always officers' relatives and friends staying, would be telephoned and asked to ensure that all officers who might be visiting it at the time received the alarm. The hurried embarkations that followed these alarms were usually watched sympathetically by a goodly part of the population of Harwich clustered round the landing steps.[12]

Surrendered German U-boats at Harwich, 1918. The graveyard of another war-winning weapon.

Harwich was the main base for submarines in the North Sea and the casualties were heavy. Some of those who hurried down the steps never came back. It was in the Stour estuary that the surrendered U-boats were interned rather than at Scapa Flow.

Harwich also became the target for Zeppelins, even after they had been forced away from London. Harwich, like Lowestoft and Yarmouth (target for the first Zeppelin raid), lived under threat for every day of the war, yet civilian casualties were much lower here than in Dover and Folkestone.

Harwich was also the port for the most regular shipping contact with Holland – the daily packet-boat was the only regular sailing to and from the UK for European neutrals. From Harwich sailed Captain Fryatt, the packet-boat captain, in a voyage that led to one of the most widely publicised tragedies of the war – he was shot by the Germans after he had been accused of ramming a German submarine. There is a fine memorial to him at Liverpool Street station, funded by admirers of Dutch nationality.

Dover, Kent

The depth charge only came later in the war, in 1917. Earlier the tactic of choice against the submarine was the indicator net, designed to snag the submarine and force it to surface. This meant a call on yet another

Dover – a key base for the Dover Patrol and for command of the Channel.

section of the fishing fleet – the drifters. On 2 January 1915, the First Lord of the Admiralty (Winston Churchill) made a request for four drifters to be sent to Dover for the special service of 'entrapping submarines'. The Scots were to come to Dover:

> The drifter is smaller than the trawler, and is usually built of wood ... she has no powerful winches and but one capstan; in lines she is but slightly modified from the old sailing drifters: and unlike the steam trawlers she relies very much on her mizzen (sail), not for speed, but sea-keeping ability in bad weather and for riding to her nets [...] The drifter crew is small and she is more often than not manned by members of one family.[13]

Echoing the Pals battalions on land were the family drifters at sea. Many were descended from families forced to the north-east coast of Scotland by the Highland clearances. The drifters had distinctive names, 'a curious mixture of Old Testament piety blended with modern ambitions and family pride. *Integrity, Breadwinner, Courage, Diligence, Direct Me, Effort, Enterprise, Faithful Friend, Friendly Star, Girl Margaret, Boy Bob, Golden Effort, Good Tidings, Hope, Peacemaker, Present Help, Protect me, Star of Faith, Sublime.*'[14] They brought their strong dissenting creeds to Dover together with the voice of the Scottish Highlands.

Releasing a depth charge from a drifter.

A permit was needed to enter the Dover area and some 22,000 of these were issued during the war. The Dover Patrol stationed there became one of the most famous formations, with a board game of the same name. Starting from a group of twelve Tribal Class destroyers it built up to a force of 300 ships, which in its range of roles and range of vessels was unique. It included trawlers, drifters and motor yachts, as well as destroyers and torpedo boats, and at the start of the war it included monitors for bombarding German troops on the Belgian coast.

It had taken forty years to build the harbour at Dover and even then it had to be finished in haste at the start of the war, but the harbour certainly proved its worth in being accessible and defensible. There were no incursions into Dover harbour and few collisions. The record was especially impressive as many shiploads of munitions were moved through Dover.

Dover was also the scene of some of the most dramatic naval incidents of the war. In April 1917 German destroyers and torpedo boats made one of their few sorties down the Channel. They were intercepted by a group of British destroyers, including *Broke*:

Despite the odds, Evans gave immediate orders to close for battle. With shells falling around them the British ships got within torpedo range and sank one ship, while the guns of both British ships put two further German ships out of action. Although sustaining serious damage herself, *Broke* sent her third victim to the bottom. (After some vicious hand-to-hand fighting.) The action had awakened the people of Dover. When they looked out to sea, it was impossible to see what was happening in the dark, but as the British destroyers limped back into port and the news flashed round the harbour, every siren and steam whistle shrieked into life. In an effort to restore some decorum, one harbour officer ordered the din to cease. The response from the trawler crews with whom Evans was particularly popular was 'Go to 'ell. It's Teddy'.[15]

Within days headlines across the country were telling the story of the *Broke* and the *Swift* and how they defied the odds to keep safe the English Channel. As Evans approached the berth he caught sight of the victualling officer: 'Have you any beer. My men are worth a gallon apiece.' However, there were six other raids where the response was less effective. Contact had to be made in darkness with ships moving at 25 knots.

Dover was also the base for the first attempt at blocking the Channel to submarines. Apart from minesweeping and repelling surface attacks, the aim of the Dover Patrol was to force German submarines to take the much longer route round the north of Scotland. There was a line of mines and nets across the Channel from the Goodwin Sands to the French coast, but this was not a success, as the strong tides kept moving the nets and submarines had little difficulty in getting under them. It was only with a changed design and a different location – between Folkestone and Gris Nez in France in 1918 – that the barrage began to work.

Dover was the target for numerous air attacks and the caves in the cliffs began to be used as shelters. It was also the transit point for the wounded with special berths for hospital ships and special links for hospital trains. These had to move to different areas of the country – often to areas where there were convalescent homes in country houses. The movement and staffing of these trains was a huge task well organised.

The port organisation of Dover was exceptional. With limited rail capacity in lines to the docks it was vital to clear ships quickly. The rail capacity was even more limited after the tunnel on the line between Folkestone and Dover was blocked by a landslip and the Treasury refused to pay for a repair. With the visitors and workers there was enormous pressure on the limited housing in the town. The port area is surrounded by a ring of hills which are almost as steep as cliffs.

Folkestone, Kent

There was less naval activity here, although on 17 February 1918 there was a destroyer raid on the now successful barrage, when 'gunfire reverberated through the narrow streets of the town'.[16] The population expanded from a peacetime 10,000 to 100,000 and every room was crammed. It was notable, too, for many thousands of Canadians in Shorncliffe and many Belgian refugees. Folkestone was a hub of activity, which made a highly effective contribution to the war effort. From the Hythe ranges, through the port and the airship station at Capel-le-Ferne, Folkestone was in the forefront. Even in the language of war the area made a significant contribution with the word 'lyddite' for explosives from Lydd, and the term 'blimp' from the sound of airship fabric being tested at Capel-le-Ferne.

As previously mentioned Folkestone was the main transit hub for the Western Front, with 7 million men going down the Road of Remembrance to the curved dock, which is still there, much as it was. The transit system was made possible by the support from Folkestone and surrounding areas, which covered maintenance and coaling of the five cross-Channel ships. This had to be done at night, as the ships were making as many as two crossings a day each. Each ship steamed around 250,000 miles in the course of the war. Coming back they brought troops on leave. In the harbour there was always a destroyer with steam up ready to take VIPs (another new expression of the time) over to France.

Scarborough, Yorkshire

On Wednesday, 16 December 1914 at 8 a.m. the first shells were fired into the resort town of Scarborough.[17] There were other raids on Hartlepool and Whitby on the same morning, but the raid on Scarborough was much more heavily publicised because the civilian casualties were higher and there were no military targets such as existed in Hartlepool.

The cruisers *Von Der Tann* and *Derfflinger* opened fire on the coast guard station, castle and disused barracks. Some shells hit the high buildings of the Grand and Royal hotels immediately along the

GERMAN RAID. DEC. 16TH. 1914.
NO.2. WYKEHAM STREET. (4 KILLED.)

No. 2 Wykeham Street where four people were killed, although the 90-year-old lodger survived.

2 Wykeham Street today.

GERMAN RAID DEC. 16TH 1914. SHELLS EXPLODING ON THE CASTLE WALLS, SCARBOROUGH.

Bombardment of the castle in Scarborough.

seafront, others went over the hotels and the station and hit houses in the residential streets behind. At No. 2 Wykeham Street Mrs Bennett, one of her sons (a Territorial) and grandson and a visiting child were killed. A 90-year-old woman lodger in the bedroom on the top floor survived: 'The old lady Mrs Edmunds (born 1824) escaped uninjured except for the shock.'[18] The family dog and a canary were killed but the family cat survived and was found three days later in a copper boiler. The bombardment of Scarborough was something new and completely unexpected. It was also a serious blow to the reputation of the First Lord of the Admiralty, Winston Churchill. The bombardment lasted twenty minutes before the cruisers turned back to the German coast. They left behind the *Kolberg*, which laid a minefield down the coast to Flamborough Head.

Liverpool, Lancashire

This was the most important port for the vital transatlantic traffic.[19] The traffic was diverted from Southampton as a result of the submarine threat south of Ireland. Liverpool became even more important in the last two years of the war and the massive size of its dock area, stretching for 19 miles along the Mersey, still impresses today. In the war every foot was occupied with unloading and transit. The road, canal and rail links were excellent.

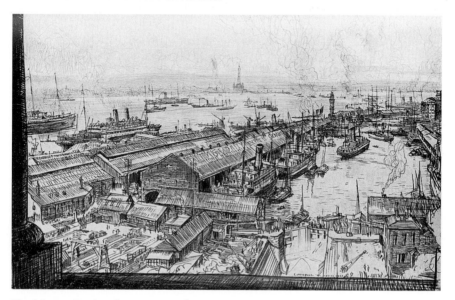

The Mersey Docks: the main British ocean-going port.

Leviathan of Liverpool. The ships got bigger as the war went on.

Seamen signing on and heading to danger.

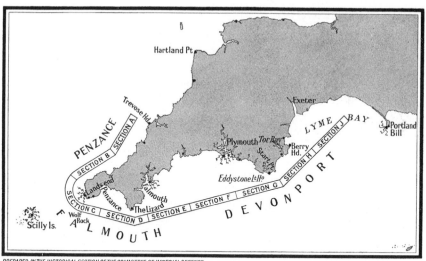

PREPARED IN THE HISTORICAL SECTION OF THE COMMITTEE OF IMPERIAL DEFENCE.

The coastal route managed from Falmouth.

Falmouth, Cornwall

This was the base for some of the 200 launches or fast motorboats (American-built) that formed the hydrophone flotilla operating out of Penzance, Falmouth and Devonport.[20] From mid-1917 there was

intensified submarine hunting along the coast up to Lyme Bay. However, even with many surface vessels it proved very hard to detect or
sink submarines. The main reason for the significant decline in the
sinking of merchant ships was the convoy system. In this first phase
the anti-submarine war had been led by destroyers farther out in the
Atlantic based at Queenstown (now Cobh) in Ireland: now the hunt
for submarines was much closer to the coast, using smaller ships to
throw depth charges.

The Nab Light, Hampshire

This tower, which is still visible off Portsmouth, replaced the Nab light-
ship in 1919.[21] It was originally built in Shoreham as a part of a pair
of towers designed to lift sunken merchant ships off the seabed. It was
never used for this and found a permanent use warning of the rocks off
the approach to Portsmouth.

Sheerness, Kent

This was the dockyard at the southern edge of the Medway estuary,
favoured by its nearness to deep water and ease of approach from the
North Sea. It was the scene of two of the worst naval accidents of the
war. On 26 November 1914 the old battleship *Bulwark* blew up while
moored in the Medway, with a loss of 736 people. This was blamed
on the overheating of cordite in shells, which had been stacked next to
a boiler room bulkhead. On 27 May 1915 the *Princess Irene*, a passenger ship (originally built for the Vancouver-Victoria-Seattle run but
requisitioned for mine-laying) blew up while anchored off the dockyard, with a loss of 275 lives. This was put down to faulty priming
of mines by inexperienced workers. It was a bigger explosion than
that of the *Bulwark* and debris were thrown 20 miles. These two accidents between them killed far more than the numbers killed by explosions in the munitions industry throughout the war. During the First
World War no civilian community suffered as much loss and damage
as Sheerness.

There is a moving memorial in the town which commemorates not
only the fallen in uniform but civilians who died in the *Princess Irene*
– mainly dockyard workers. The high dockyard walls are still there,
although everything in the original Blue Town (so-called because of
the use of borrowed Admiralty blue paint in the eighteenth century)

has disappeared except for the name. The heritage centre is close to the large pubs that ringed the walls of the dockyard in numbers, each one with a name more patriotic than the last. The gas jet used for lighting pipes as workers left the yard is still there, as is the wall.

Notes

1 Salter, J.A., *Allied Shipping Control: An Experiment in International Administration*, Oxford University Press, 1921, p. 123.
2 Raleigh, W., *The War in the Air*, Vol. 1, Oxford, 1922, pp. 208–9.
3 Salter, op. cit., p. 123.
4 Newbolt, H., *History of the Great War: Naval Operations*, Vol. V, Longman, 1931, pp. 141–2.
5 Halpern, P.G., *A Naval History of World War 1*, Naval Insitute Press, 1994, pp. 405–10.
6 Marder, A.J., *From the Dreadnought to Scapa Flow: The Royal Navy in the Fisher Era, 1904–1919*, Pen and Sword, Vol. 1, 2013.
7 Hurd, Archibald, *History of The Great War: The Merchant Navy*, Vol. 1, John Murray, 1921, pp. 257–8.
8 Pratt, op. cit., p. 513.
9 Hewison, W.S., *This Great Harbour Scapa Flow*, The Orkney Press, 1985, p. 39.
10 Jellicoe, Viscount, *The Grand Fleet 1914–16*, Cassell, 1919, pp. 297–8.
11 Patterson, A., *Temple, Tyrwhitt of the Harwich Force*, Military Book Society, 1973, p. 146.
12 Patterson, loc. cit., p. 146.
13 Hurd, A., op cit., pp. 372–3.
14 Ibid, pp. 373.
15 George, M. and C., *Dover and Folkestone During the Great War*, Pen and Sword, 2008, p. 109.
16 Carlile, J.C., loc. cit., p. 298.
17 Clarke, Bob, *Remember Scarborough*, Amberley, 2010.
18 Anon, *The German Raid on Scarborough 1914*, E.T.W. Dennis, p. 42.
19 Bone, D.W., *Merchantmen-at-Arms*, Chatto and Windus, 1929, p. 146.
20 Newbolt, H., op. cit., pp. 194–204.
21 Munro, D.J., *Convoys, Blockades and Mystery Towers*, Sampson Low and Marston, 1932, p. 192.

7

The Air War

In 1914 the Royal Flying Corps had 150 aircraft; by November 1918 there were 22,000 and 300,000 personnel in the RAF. Over England (there was one Zeppelin attack on Scotland and none on Wales) the offensive in the air war was by the Germans. The British developments were to counter a series of threats by Zeppelins and Gotha bombers. The counter-measures were successful, stopping the threat from growing or blocking it entirely, as in the case of Zeppelins, so that the Zeppelin branch was abolished in 1917. From a very small beginning the British won the air war and also achieved a worldwide lead by setting up the first independent air force, the RAF, which pioneered the distinctive three-coloured roundel later copied by many of the world's air forces.

The British effort was designed to meet a specific air-attack threat – there was little sense yet of airpower as a massive new force that would change warfare forever. It was the Germans who pinned most hopes on the effects of bombing raids in starting a fire storm that would consume half of London; however, the means available did not make this feasible.

Aeroplane development was one of the few areas of inter-Allied cooperation in weapons-making. Some 80 per cent of the engines used in the British-made aircraft were of French design. The Sopwith Camel, the most successful British plane of the war, had a Clerget engine, made under licence in Lincoln. France had been leading the design and manufacture of aircraft before 1914 and continued this initiative, particularly with regard to engine making. Unlike the other new weapons – tanks, guns and chemical warfare – there was genuine cooperation in aircraft production, which was vital to the British effort in the air.

The Zeppelin raid of 13–14 October 1915 was the most successful raid on central London.

The two bombing campaigns, first by Zeppelins and then by Gotha bombers, were political as well as military events. The Zeppelin raids were frequent and these airships spent long periods over the UK. They were highly visible, as they operated on clear nights and they visited not just London but many other industrial centres, bringing the war home to industrial England. The blackout was vital in blinding the Zeppelins even before it became possible to shoot them down in 1916. Numerous attempts were made to bomb Leeds but the closest bombs fell harmlessly on Roundhay and Harewood: 'Leeds escaped danger largely if not entirely because it was enveloped in darkness on every occasion when an alarm was given.'[1] For the first year there was nothing that could be done, as the Zeppelins were flying higher than most British aircraft. The presence of these great craft in the sky was a national humiliation. After the middle of 1916 the coming of the Sopwith Pup, with a faster rate of climb, and the phosphorus bullet that could ignite the hydrogen in the balloon, completely changed the challenge. In the meantime, the air issue created the first great populist in the independent MP Noel Pemberton Billing, air power apologist and unhinged conspiracy theorist.

The air war had greater social than military effects. According to the official history:

> The air-raid menace, more, perhaps than any other aspect of the war, was responsible for a temporary revolution in English social and general life. Night brought the unrelieved gloom of darkened streets and a brooding sense of danger.[2]

During the raid of 23–24 September 1916:

> ... many thousands of people flocked to the tube railways without waiting for any warning. Many of them began to take up their places about 5.30 p.m. prepared to camp out until the danger, real or imaginary, was over. They went in family parties and carried with them, pillows, bedding, provisions and family parties.[3]

The raids did cause industrial disruption because of the need to extinguish blast furnaces, and they also diverted men, guns and aeroplanes from the Western Front. By the end of 1917 there were 17,341 people specifically retained in England for home anti-aircraft defence.

The original German plan was for attacking waves of 120 planes returning nightly, but this was not to be. Thus the degree of precaution reflected an understandable uncertainty, as well as the reality of the situation.

After the Zeppelins the Gotha raids were a massive shock. They dropped heavier bombs than the Zeppelins and caused more civilian casualties. In fact, half of all the UK casualties were caused by three raids in 1917: on Folkestone; the East End, including Poplar School; and

Chatham Barracks, where 123 naval cadets were killed. However, the blockade had limited the materials available and the Gothas were often unreliable because of poor workmanship and poor-quality fuel. They were also limited in number with rarely more than twenty available.

The Gotha raids, however, caused great shock, not least to the Royal family. The naming of the Gotha bomber caused a change from the House of Saxe-Coburg-Gotha to the House of Windsor. Bad weather and anti-aircraft guns often forced the Gothas to stop short of London and seek easier targets on the coast. While there were only three heavy raids on the capital, there was still a high degree of public alarm and hundreds of thousands sheltered in Underground stations.

As with Zeppelins the political impact was greater than the strategic impact. The air war led to a sense of threat and vulnerability, which may also help to explain the unusual softening of inter-service rivalry with the concentration of both army and navy air activities in the new RAF. The long-term consequences were certainly positive, with a strong momentum in development extending through to the 1930s and the birth of the Spitfire. On land, future British governments would try to move as far away as possible from the Great War templates, but in the air there was greater continuity. Thus the political tensions caused by the Gotha raids had long-term consequences.

In *The Times History of the War*, a twenty-one-volume account published in 1919, there was in fact very little about the air war, and virtually nothing about the air war on the Western Front. The Zeppelin raids in 1915 and onwards received most attention. There were fifty raids, beginning with the first on Yarmouth on 19–20 January. Zeppelins were prone to navigation errors and often the crews themselves did not know where they were. The real military impact of the air war was in fact on the Western Front:

> War in the air demands a quickness of thought and nerve greater than is exacted by any other kind of war. It is a deadly and gallant tournament. The airman goes out to seek his enemy: he must be full of initiative. His ordeal may come upon him suddenly at any time, with less than a minute's notice: he must be able to concentrate all his powers instantaneously to meet it. He fights alone. During a great part of his time in the air he is in easy reach of safety; a swift glide will take him far away from the enemy, but he must choose danger, and carry on.[4]

Along with the sudden stress of aerial combat was the continuous daily activity of photographic reconnaissance, recorded in the Royal Flying

"Thawing out

A pilot thawing out. The cold endured by airmen was often atrocious.

Corps weekly communiqués. It was air reconnaissance, not gladiatorial fighter combat, that made aircraft so important. Aerial location of batteries was essential to success in the artillery duel and the aces were there to protect the slower reconnaissance planes against marauders.

The invention by the Dutchman Anthony Fokker of the interrupter gear, by which machine guns could be fired through the propeller, gave the German Air Force a period of superiority in 1915–16 – the marauders ruled the skies. The threat led to the development of the Sopwith Pup and the Sopwith Camel.

The main day-to-day activity of the Royal Flying Corps was to take photographs. The air arm made its greatest contribution by improving artillery effectiveness and then, increasingly in 1918, in ground-attack on infantry. As the official history put it:

> Air fighting was waged to win freedom of movement for the reconnaissance, photographic, bombing and artillery aeroplanes in their essential task of helping the Army to overcome the enemy, and to deny similar freedom to the opposing air service.[5]

The German Reichsarchiv set it on record that the British infantry successes on the Somme were due to the 'unquestionable superiority' of the British air co-operation with the artillery. This involved radio contact by which planes gave batteries locations of targets and checked accuracy of fire:

> What made the air and artillery co-operation so important during the battle was that the undulating uplands of the Somme shielded most important targets, even near the front line trenches, from any observation on the ground. Aerial photographs made it possible to identify trench lines and supply routes as well as batteries. Experience in the reading of aerial photographs had shown that they might be exploited to reveal considerably more than the positions of trenches and strong points. With a map of the area in front of him, the expert first of all visualises the configuration and nature of the ground. He then notes the direction of the light at the time when the photograph was taken [...] The important military features he looks for are battery positions, trench mortar and machine-gun emplacements, snipers' posts, tracks, trolley lines, headquarters, telephone exchanges, wire and so forth. Nothing gives a fuller insight into the daily lives of troops than tracks, for they are almost impossible of concealment.[6]

For three months on the Somme in 1916 such was the Allied air superiority that no German aircraft could cross the line, thus they were denying information to the Germans that was available hourly to themselves.

From 1917 onwards the Royal Flying Corps had a new role in dropping propaganda leaflets. A German Foreign Office note of 22 May 1917 stated that British aircraft had recently dropped 'inflammatory writings, some in particular directed against His Majesty the German Emperor and those acts were in the opinion of the German government, outside the scope of acts of war'. Pilots were threatened with execution. In 1918 millions of leaflets were distributed over the German lines by unmanned balloons.

Other developments, such as the emergence of long-distance bombing, were dramatic but had little effect on the war. The assessment of the First World War air activities is somewhat overshadowed by the events of the Second World War.

Yarmouth, Norfolk

The Royal Naval Air Service (RNAS) played an important role in reconnaissance and then in convoy protection, and used some airships as well as seaplanes; the main seaplane base at Great Yarmouth monitored the North Sea.[7] The role of seaplanes was limited by weather and their weak armament. They were more difficult to fly than conventional planes and had to be made of stronger materials for sea conditions, which made the frame heavier. Both landing and take-off required unusual skills and pilots who learned to fly on land could not transfer to seaplanes without further extensive training. The seaplanes were also liable to engine failure, which often left the crews stranded far out in the North Sea. They could only take off in reasonable weather and there were many weeks (as recorded in the Yarmouth station logs) when the weather was too bad for flying.

The seaplanes had to settle for reconnaissance. Here they played a vital role in giving early warning of hostile forces. However, they could not fly high enough or fast enough to catch the Zeppelins that flew over the bases in East Anglia on their way to London. Instead, the seaplanes were given the role of escorting convoys, which seems to have been quite effective in deterring U-boats, as their presence could be reported by wireless, but they were not able to hunt or sink the U-boats when they identified them. German air activities over the sea suffered from the same problems.

The seaplane station at Great Yarmouth. Seaplanes were difficult to fly, often making them more dangerous to the pilot than to the enemy.

Thus serving in seaplanes was dangerous and must have been frustrating, so the RNAS turned to the development of carriers. The carrier raids on the Zeppelin bases at Tondern 1918 were launched from the first purpose-built carrier and there were also experiments with launching aerial torpedoes. The RNAS contributed vitally to the success of the North Sea blockade but it was limited by the offensive power of the aircraft. As on land, technology did not meet aspiration.

The RAE Farnborough, Hampshire

This had been established before 1914 as the main centre for aeroplane development and it was here that Samuel Cody had made the first manned flight in the UK. It was the Woolwich of the air, providing most of the standards and some of the designs for the expansion of aircraft production.

Sopwith, Kingston, London

This factory was founded by yet another American migrant, Thomas Sopwith, in a converted ice rink by the Thames. And it was where most of the successful Sopwith Camels were built. The Camel – so-named because of the humps over which the two machine guns were

RAE Farnborough

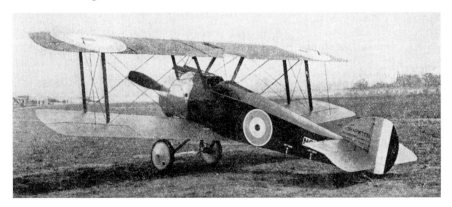

The Sopwith Camel-built in Kingston – the pick of the 22,000 RAF aircraft.

mounted – was difficult to fly but reckoned by experienced pilots to be the 'supreme dogfighting machine'. Its handling characteristics 'were a gift to the experienced pilot but could kill the slow and unwary'. As one ace put it:

> A skilled pilot could not wish for a better mount. To him it was like having a pair of wings strapped onto his shoulder blades. They were wonderful in a dogfight because they could make the quickest change of direction of any machine that flew in the War.

The airframe cost £875 and the French Clerget 9B engine, built under licence, cost £910.[9] The German Air Force had some highly effective aces, but through formation flying and superior numbers Sopwith Camels won air superiority.

Gosport, Hampshire

Grange Airfield was the place where systematic improvements in pilot training were made. There had been many justified complaints about inexperienced pilots being thrown into combat in 1916: the Gosport school brought in systematic methods that are still the basis of flying training. The Gosport system of training 'was based not on avoiding potentially dangerous manoeuvres (as had been the case before) but on exposing the student to them in a controlled manner so that he could learn to recover from them, thereby gaining confidence and skill'.[10] Students were able to use purpose-built aircraft, the Avro 504J, which had dual controls and inflight communication by means of a length of soft rubber tubing, the Gosport tube. For the first time military pilots flew into action as masters of their aeroplanes.[11]

Norwich, Norfolk

Boulton and Paul produced 1,600 Sopwith Pup airframes. The Clerget 9B engines were made under licence in Lincoln by Ruston and Proctor. Thus, once again, the East of England made a vital contribution in the new phase of munitions production.

Cuffley, Hertfordshire

It was here in Hertfordshire on the night of 3 September 1916 that a Zeppelin – actually an Army Schutte-Lanz Airship SL11 – was shot down.[12] (The local football team is still nicknamed 'the Zeps' after this event.) This was the first airship to be shot down, helped by much improved searchlighting so that the Zeppelins were caught by the beams. It was also the first use of incendiary bullets, which could ignite the hydrogen in the balloon. Lieutenant Leefe Robinson was flying a BE2C biplane with an open cockpit and top speed of 70mph, so it was a remarkable feat to climb to 10,000ft and get close enough to the SL11 to fire three drums of ammunition. The airship fell near the current Plough Inn, near Cuffley, and there is a memorial in East Ridgeway to Leefe Robinson (who died in November 1918 after a year as a prisoner of war).

Memorial to Captain Robinson at Cuffley in Hertfordshire.

Sutton's Farm, Essex
(later Hornchurch RAF Station)

This was the main aerodrome for fighters in the defence of London and it was here that the successful attacks against Zeppelins began. Lieutenant William Leefe Robinson took off from here for the first victorious attack over Cuffley, Hertfordshire, in 1917.

Potters Bar, Hertfordshire

On 2 October 1916, L31 was shot down over Potters Bar 2 miles west of Cuffley.[13] It was picked out by searchlights and tried to escape the beams but without success. 'Lieutenant Tempest was flying higher and faster than the Zeppelin and was able to close in and despatch a succession of incendiary bullets into its massive frame.' Some of the crew jumped as the flames took hold. The captain, Lieutenant Mathy, is buried in the Cannock Chase German War Cemetery. Mathy had held the record for the most bombing raids on England. This scene was watched by many thousands of Londoners, including a young journalist: 'When at last the doomed airship vanished from sight, there arose a shout the like of which I never heard in London before – a swelling shout that appeared to be rising from all parts of the metropolis, ever increasing in force and intensity.' On 4 October there were 50,000 visitors to the site.

Tempest Avenue is in Potters Bar, close to the crash site. The site of the Zeppelin oak, cut down in 1958, is at (demolished) 9–11 Tempest Avenue. There is a useful notice about the crash in Oakmere Park nearby, together with a war memorial, unusual in that the names of the fallen are picked out (at the expense of the normally frugal citizens of Hertfordshire) in gold lettering.

Lieutenant Tempest's feat depended on individual initiative. He did not stay on his allocated beat or at the official maximum height of 8,000ft. He and some of his colleagues had, in fact, practised flying higher so that they were able to climb to the Zeppelin height of 12,000ft. Motivation had been increased by reading a letter from Lieutenant Mathy to the *New York Times* in September, threatening to 'smash London on the first day of October'.

Bolton, Lancashire

This was the scene of an attack by Zeppelin L21 on the night of 26 September 1916.[14] The highest number of casualties was in Kirk Street. Here five explosive bombs completely destroyed six terraced houses, killing thirteen people and seriously injuring nine. The *Bolton Chronicle* reported that:

> In the part of the town where the most severe damage was wrought, four bombs crashed below in rapid succession on a populous working class neighbourhood [...] And death only too truly took 12 humble lives of men, women and babies in this one unfortunate street. Pitifully pathetic was the death of a mother (Mrs Joseph Irwin) and her 2-year-old baby which was clasped tightly to her breast. Pathetic too was the fate of a man and his wife (Mr and Mrs Mcdermott) and 6-year-old child in the house next door, who were all overwhelmed in the ruins of their home.

Most of the funerals were held in the local Catholic church as the bombs seemed to have struck streets mainly occupied by migrants from Ireland. The Zeppelin had travelled over the town for some

The west side of Kirk Street looking towards Dean Road after the Zeppelin raid on Bolton on 26 September 1916.

minutes and had circled twice, before flying off to the north and returning to Germany, dropping a bomb on Skipton on the way. L21 was shot down on 28 November, over the North Sea off Lowestoft, using the new incendiary bullets. This was the last raid until the new high-flying Zeppelins were introduced. One of these carried out a raid on Wigan on 12 April 1918, which killed five people. Given the intense fighting then current on the Western Front, this raid did not get as much attention as the earlier one.

Children leave flowers at the graves of their dead playmates after the Folkestone raid of 25 May 1917.

Folkestone, Kent

On 25 May 1917 there was the first raid by the new Gotha bombers. The 'distinctive double note of the engines – troops described it as the Gotha hum – caused more and more people to look up at the sky'.[15] The bombers had to turn back from London because of heavy cloud and instead dropped their bombs on Folkestone. One fell on the Canadians at Shorncliffe, preparing for an evening exercise, killing seventeen and wounding ninety-three. Twenty high-explosive and thirty anti-personnel bombs were then dropped on Folkestone, most landing on Tontine Street, a busy shopping street on a Friday evening: 'Everywhere lay the dead and dying, while the moans and cries of the injured echoed through the ruined streets.'[16]

Upper North Street, London

On 13 June twenty-two Gothas launched the first raid to reach London. It was a clear day and thousands of people gazed up 'wonderstruck at the sight of the pure-white Gothas, silvered by the

morning sunlight and hovering like hawks over a dovecot'. A pilot
later reported:

> Visibility over London was unusually clear and all details could be
> made out with ease. Stations, factories and warehouses looked like
> pieces in a game. Further to the east, on the main tributaries and
> canals leading to the Thames, large shipyards and docks unfurled.
> Out of the formless masses of stone and brick, the sinister fortress
> of the Tower, St Paul's Cathedral and the Bank of England were
> unmistakable landmarks. What panic and fear of death was now
> gripping these people in the sea of houses far below us as they
> desperately searched for protection and cover? But though they
> were like us and of our blood, we could not think about the people
> who lived in this metropolis. We were at war after all, total war that
> demanded all our strength and resolve.[17]

The daylight raid on London in July 1917, part of the Gotha raid. The raiders, owing
to their great height, had an appearance of a flock of birds.

Bombs were dropped on Liverpool Street Station and other bombs fell on the Royal Albert Dock and on a building in Fenchurch Street. Eighteen children were killed at Upper North Street School in Poplar. The raiders had spent ninety minutes in British airspace, unloading 4 tons of bombs on London, killing 162 people and injuring 432.

The next raid, on 4 July, killed fewer people but devastated the Central Telegraph Office at St Martin's Le Grand. In three abortive raids during August, the England Squadron failed to reach London and lost twenty-one aircraft, partly due to bad weather, but mainly because of attacks by fighters. The Gotha performance was also affected by poor quality of construction:

> Inspection of our planes shot down on the other side had indicated to them that as we had no more copper and rubber (which was in such short supply that the army had even requisitioned the cushions from German billiard tables) that welding work on our steel spars was faulty, that our fuel – a benzo-alcohol mixture – often contained so much water that the engines began to cough.[18]

London Underground

On 24 September 1917 the Gothas began attacks at night. On the night of the first raid of the Blitz of the Harvest Moon a concourse estimated that 100,000 people had rushed to take shelter in the Underground:

> Everywhere working women looked exhausted from sleeplessness, anxiety and fear. Each night at this time, queues formed outside the Tube Station waiting to go down if an alarm was given [...] The sights in the Tube were the most extraordinary imaginable [...] women were dressing on the platforms, and taking their hair out of curling pins; some were pulling on their stockings [...] The staircase and platforms of the Tube stations were like a huge bedroom and night nursery.[19]

The six raids in the Blitz of the Harvest Moon had caused panic and Londoners' nerves were frayed, but bad weather and a shortage of usable aircraft meant this was the last series of major raids, as the German air arm did not have the resources to follow up.

Notes

1 Scott, W.H., *Leeds in the Great War*, op. cit., p. 43.

2 Jones, H.A., *The War in the Air*, Vol. III, Oxford, 1931, p. 247.

3 Hanson, N., *First Blitz*, Doubleday, 2008.

4 Raleigh, W., *The War in the Air*, Vol. I, Oxford, 1922, pp. 209–1.

5 Ibid.

6 Ibid.

7 Snowden Gamble, C.F., *The Story of a North Sea Air Station*, Oxford University Press, 1928.

8 Jones, *The War in the Air*, p. 143.

9 RAF Museum. There is a very good display here on the Sopwith Camel.

10 Gosport. Website on Grange Airfield, 2013.

11 Ibid.

12 Jones, *The War in the Air*, p. 225.

13 Ibid, pp. 236–8.

14 Smith, Peter J.C., *Zeppelins Over Lancashire*, N. Richardson, 1991, pp. 16–22.

15 Hanson, *First Blitz*.

16 Ibid, p. 68.

17 Ibid, p. 88.

18 Ibid.

19 Jones, *The War in the Air*, p. 247.

8

Medical and Health Services

The medical services were a large investment and one that had some success in containing further costs from disease. Such a gigantic conflict as the First World War fought relentlessly in such poor conditions would have had a second series of losses beyond the military in terms of disease and worsening health.

For health services the First World War was a short, forced transition that completely changed the way health services worked. In the phrase of a widely read review published in 1919 it was 'The Triumph of the Doctor'.[1] *The Times History of the War* gave far more space to the medical services than it did to the air war.

The medical services were widely regarded as by far the best organisation in the First World War. They owed a great deal to the ability of Sir Alfred Keogh. The RAMC was founded in 1898 and Major Keogh (as he was in 1899) rapidly rose to become director as a Major General in 1905. He was responsible for the basic reorganisation of the services so that the duties of the medical officer were widened to cover all aspects of sanitation. He introduced a research programme based at Netley, Hampshire, and built the RAMC College at Milbank next to the Tate Gallery. He also introduced the Territorial Army medical service and planned for the secondment of leading doctors to the RAMC in wartime. Lord Haldane's tribute was deserved: 'The country owes much to Sir Alfred Keogh for his insight and devoted labours.'[2]

The new systems included his use of managed medical research, the extension of surgery through teamwork, wider employment of X-rays and anaesthetics, along with the use of dental, optical and rehabilitation services. Services such as dentistry, which had been used by the

TOMMY AND HIS "FAGS."

PIPE MAY BE FORCED TO OUST THE CIGARETTE.

SMOKE SUSPICION.

QUESTION AUTHORITIES ARE CONSIDERING.

("ECHO" SPECIAL.)

An officer of the R.A.M.C., on holiday in Liverpool, told an "Echo" representative that the soldiers' habits were likely to be transformed by a special report which is now being made by Army doctors on the vitality of the smoking versus the non-smoking soldier.

There are few soldiers who do not smoke. The majority of soldiers smoke what are popularly known as "fags," and the sale of cigarettes reaches the enormous number of at least two hundred millions per week. It is certain that the reason why our export trade in tobacco has increased since the war began is through the enormous number of cigarettes sent to the boys at the front.

Yet it has occurred to a cold, unemotional doctor, "somewhere at the front" to make a comparison in his sick returns of the number of pipe-smokers who speedily recovered from their wounds, the number of cigarette-smokers, and the number who did not smoke at all.

As a result of this inquiry it has been proved that the non-smoking soldier barely exists; the pipe-smokers easily recover under ordinary circumstances, and the cigarette-smoker invariably suffers from heart failure, which "sends him under" far sooner, either in case of wounds or illness, than the man with a clay pipe or a briar.

If the Army Council decides that Tommy Atkins must do without his "fag" and take to a pipe, or else do without a smoke at all, it will play havoc with the great American Tobacco Trust, which sends billions of cigarettes to this country each year.

The whole question resolves itself into this— the war is telling us what type of habits makes for the highest form of physical fitness. The excessive alcohol drinker has been badly left in the race for physical efficiency. Once we get the complete returns from the various hospitals of the Allied armies as to which type of soldier recovers the soonest from his wounds, then we shall know who is the healthier, the pipe or the cigarette smoker.

On the result of the report depends a possible revolution affecting at least one thousand millions of capital. The employer always wants the highest possible efficiency from his employee. In the United States for many years past it has been a commonplace thing to see advertisements in the newspapers for men to take up positions which needed brains, commonsense, and energy.

Yet the advertisement always concluded with these ominous words, "Cigarette smokers need not apply"!

So we can rest assured that any order which the Army Council may make on the subject will affect not only the Army, but also civilian life.

Tommy and his 'Fags', Liverpool *Echo*, 10 February 1916. They were years ahead of their time.

better off, became available to the army. For the first time many soldiers were fitted with glasses.

The biggest commitment of the services was naturally in treatment of the wounded. In spite of the pre-war improvements made by the RAMC the services in 1914–15 were quite inadequate, with wounded men lying in hundreds on straw at the Channel ports waiting for transport. One nursing sister wrote:

> What an indescribable scene! In the first huge shed there were hundreds of walking wounded: as long as a man could crawl he had to be a walking case. All were caked in mud, in torn clothes, hardly any caps and with bloodstained bandages on hands, arms and legs. Many were lying asleep in the straw that had been left in the hastily cleared sheds, looking weary to death; others were sitting on empty boxes or barrels, eating the contents of a tin of 'maconochie' with the help of a clasp knife.[3]

The next year brought improvement based on the aim of surgery or treatment as close as possible to the front line in Casualty Clearing Stations, followed by evacuation to a base hospital in Etaples or Boulogne. Of the 1.8 million wounded, some 1.5 million recovered sufficiently to take up some military duty and of the 3.5 million sick, 3 million returned to military duty. Thus the medical services played a vital role in preserving manpower. By 1918 the manpower reserve was exhausted, but without the medical services this point would have been reached much earlier. The collapse of the German medical services was indeed one reason why Germany reached its manpower and morale limit in 1918.

Ninety per cent of the wounded who reached the Casualty Clearing Stations survived,[4] reflecting the great expertise acquired by surgical teams, success in preventing wound infections and the high standard of nursing. During the 1917 Passchendaele offensive surgeons carried out 61,000 operations; by the end of the war the nurse's role had expanded, with several hundred being trained as nurse anaesthetists. There was assistance from access to pathology and X-rays. The RAMC introduced mobile laboratories and mobile X-ray units and also brought into France the leading medical specialists, including a pathologist, Alexander Fleming, the physician Wilmot Herringham and the surgeon Berkeley Moynihan from Leeds. General Keogh (on leave from his post as rector of Imperial College), as head of the RAMC based in London, and Lieutenant General Sir Arthur Sloggett, who was in charge in France, exemplified the fact that the medical veterans were driving a remark-

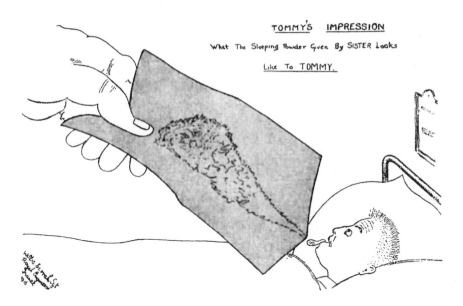

TOMMY'S IMPRESSION

What The Sleeping Powder Given By SISTER Looks

Like To TOMMY.

A soldier's view of the nursing system.

able expansion and transformation of the medical services.[5] They also benefited from rapid international collaboration with the French and Americans. The success in treating shock was due to Dr George Crile of the Cleveland Clinic, from experience gained in treating streetcar injuries in Cleveland, and the American neurosurgeon Harvey Cushing, who served as chief of neurosurgery for the RAMC. There was also collaboration with the French in adopting their invention of the steel helmet and in developing the Carrel Dakin solution for wound cleansing, after the failure of earlier attempts at using Listerian methods of pouring disinfectant into the wound. There was more allied collaboration in the medical services than in weapons development.

Fleming made an artificial wound out of glass 'using the glass blowing skills that were so useful in the laboratory and which in peacetime he had used to make glass animals for the amusement of children'.[6] He was able to show that disinfectant did not kill all the bacteria in the glass crevasses. 'Thus he demonstrated how antiseptics could not penetrate the jagged edges of the wounds of modern warfare with the result that the bacteria had an open road into the wound and could multiply unchecked in its irregular edges.' The only antiseptic that proved to be any good was Carrel-Dakin solution containing sodium hypochlorite, which soon lost its antiseptic qualities when poured on a wound and turned into saline solution, as advocated by Wright and Fleming all along.

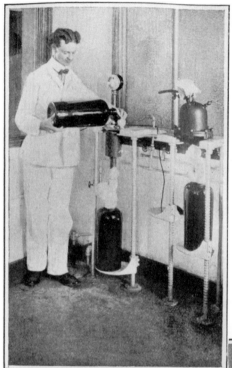

Making tetanus serums at St Mary's. The serums were pioneered by Sir Almroth Wright, who saved thousands of lives with them.

Older men volunteer for an experiment in infection by lice for trench fever. The experiment failed because their skins were too thick.

There had to be rapid adaptation to new problems. In the first stages there were the foreseeable problems of rapid infections, as recruits were brought together from different areas. The Canadians suffered an epidemic of meningitis on Salisbury Plain, but typhoid was avoided by an effective inoculation campaign led by Almroth Wright of St Mary's Hospital. One thousand British soldiers died from typhoid (mostly among the few who had avoided inoculation) and later estimates were that without the programme some 120,000 would have died. The fighting in Flanders, in heavily manured soil, led to a great danger of tetanus. Wounded men were given an immediate anti-tetanus injection as soon as they reached the advance dressing station.

Later came the problems of a long-term siege in appalling ground and weather conditions. The first problem was that of trench foot caused by damp, although this was greatly reduced by the use of Vaseline ointment, regular changes of socks and foot inspections. Later came trench fever, which was traced, after much research, to louse bites.[7] This particularly affected young conscripts in 1918, as the skin of the older soldiers was too tough even for the Flanders louse. Trials were carried out with elderly volunteers at the Royal Free Hospital in London where they were left for the night under blankets with 400 lice, yet none were infected because the lice could not bite into the thicker and drier skins of the elderly volunteers – this was a young man's disease.

The great success of the medical services was in prevention. Day to day the main guardian of health was rigorous sanitation and the RAMC introduced permanent sanitary detachments,[8] maintaining a rigorous programme of cleaning and incineration. The mobile pathology laboratories were able to give rapid answers to new threats from the 'invisible enemy', the microbe.

The regimental medical officer (RMO) played a key role in health and morale.[9] In the trenches the RMO began a daily service of sick parade, and routines were established for purifying water, fumigating clothes and ensuring regular bathing during rotation out of the line. It was the RMO who had to deliver results and by the second year cases of trench foot were rare. Laundry and bathing were assisted by the development of special bathing centres, using old brewery vats, and the labour of French civilians for washing clothes. During combat the RMO established an aid post far forward and organised stretcher bearers to bring in the wounded. The risks were heavy and the courage extraordinary. By 1917 so many RMOs had been killed, including Captain Chavasse, the only double VC of the war, that they had to be replaced by volunteer American medical officers, By the end of 1917 there were 1,200 American doctors attached to the forward troops.[10]

The success in reducing losses from disease was such that while in earlier wars there could be five deaths from diseases for every one in battle, now there was one death from disease for everyone five in battle. The 'triumph of the doctor' depended on logistics and support from across the UK:

> Our armies in Flanders and Northern France in the winter of 1917–18 out in open trenches in some of the vilest and sickliest weather troops had ever had to face, had less sickness and fewer deaths from pneumonia and all other diseases than soldiers used to have in barracks in time of peace, and far less than the general civil population at home.
>
> Inoculation protected them against typhoid; splendid feeding with plenty of meat and fat, against pneumonia and consumption; fly campaigns against dysentery and diarrhoea; shower baths and clean underwear against spotted typhus ...[11]

The attrition factor was not just about the fallen, it was about fighting capacity, which could decline, and which depended on morale and material support. There were indicators of the state of an army: the prisoner rate (the willingness to surrender); the desertion rate (Colonel Fuller, in his evidence to the shell-shock enquiry, pointed to November

1916 in the Ancre valley as the low point of British morale, and the only time that there were a significant number of deserters[12]); and the sickness rate (disease brought about partly by self neglect or reckless behaviour). These indicators rose for the French Army in 1917 and most strikingly for the German Army in 1918, but not for the British Army. The medical services bought time in the battle against war exhaustion.

The doctors also played a key role in recruitment standards. The Ministry of National Service report on 2.4 million conscripts in 1916–18 showed that only 36 per cent could be classified 'Type A', even though the standard set was low. By the end of the war recruits were being classified as Type A when they had one-quarter normal sight in one eye, so long as the sight in the other could be brought up to half-normal standard by the use of glasses.[13]

The medical services at sea faced special problems both in maintaining morale and treating casualties. On ships there were special problems of ventilation and long periods in dock led to a decline in morale. Casualties had to be winched up in special stretchers from lower decks and there were serious problems with burns in confined spaces. The Royal Navy doctors managed an effective preventive service.[14]

There was less progress in dealing with the new problems raised by war in the air.[15] There was extreme cold and lack of oxygen to contend with and only towards the end of the war was there some use of oxygen masks and cylinders, largely ineffective. Selection for pilot training was made from a long line of would-be applicants. Early on, selection was often based on horsemanship or team games, later came more defined standards in physical fitness. An elusive quality of 'flying ability', or touch, was vital for survival – sometimes the perfectly qualified and mentally stable crashed, while the psychopaths became aces. In the absence of instruments, 'feel' for the aircraft was vital.

RAMC, Milbank, London

This building, now occupied by the Chelsea College of Art and Design, was part of a large campus that included a parade ground and the Officers' Mess, reputed, pre-war, to be the best in London. It was the site of the Royal Army Medical College and there was also a Commandant's House.

During the war teaching was suspended and the college was used for the production of vaccines. It was here that most of the 10 million doses of typhoid vaccine were produced. Sir Alfred Keogh returned as director in wartime and was based at the main War Office.

St Mary's Hospital, Paddington, London

Sir Almroth Wright was a professor here with a team that included a young assistant – who had qualified in medicine after working for several years as a shipping clerk – Dr Alexander Fleming. In 1914 typhoid inoculation was made a condition for overseas service. The British Army lost 1,000 lives to typhoid compared with 40,000 French soldiers who died. An American tribute in 1915 was to 'Sir Almroth Wright who stands alone in preventive medicine. It was Wright's genius more than that of any other that was sustaining the health of the twelve to fifteen million troops on the battlefields of Europe.'[16] Wright acted as chief pathologist on the Western Front.

Blackpool, Lancashire

It was here that RAMC personnel, including Australians and Canadians, were trained and later their American colleagues. Most RAMC members were not doctors but staff with specific skills, such as the use of stretchers, first aid, management of movement in trains, ships and barges, medical assistants and sanitation workers. Some 100,000 RAMC staff were trained at Blackpool and Leeds for later service in France. These skills helped minimise worsening of injuries during transport, first by stretcher then by ambulance. They also gave the injured immediate help in reducing blood loss, giving tetanus injections and cleansing and bandaging wounds. They were under the command of the battalion medical officer but they had to show much initiative in dealing with desperate problems of haemorrhage, pain and shock. These were the first responders.

The British official histories deal mainly with the doctor-led services and the hospitals behind the lines, whereas the Australian histories are unusual in paying tribute to these front-liners. The stretcher bearer was the first on-hand to help a wounded man lying alone, immobile and perhaps even unable to use the bandage in his kit. As Australian history states: 'even if he does not speak a word, with a pair of strong arms he can raise a man from hell to heaven in half an hour.'[17] Sometimes this was done in no-man's-land under a white flag, as on the Somme, but more often under fire.

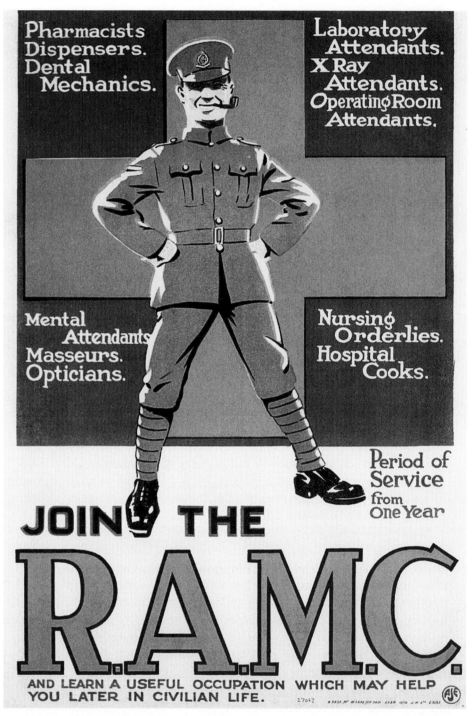

The Royal Army Medical Corps' confidence grew after the war, as this advertisement shows.

Woolwich, London

This was the site of the main centre for bandages and medical supply. It was not just the beer supply that surprised the German stormtroopers in the March 1918 offensive but the vast quantity of medical supplies, including bandages, splints and morphine, at a time when the German services had no morphine and had to make do with paper bandages.[18] Woolwich was the main centre for contracting supplies and organising their distribution among several hundred hospitals and casualty clearing stations. As the war progressed, the range of medical and surgical equipment became much greater, with more extensive use of X-rays and blood transfusions.

Endell Street, London

This was the first hospital in the world to be staffed entirely by women doctors. These included specialists such as surgeons (Dr Winifred Buckley), ophthalmologists (Dr Amy Sheppard) and pathologists (Dr Helen Chambers). The hospital specialised in complex surgery:

> The surgeons spent all their mornings in the wards, and most of their afternoons in the operating theatre, where it was not unusual to have a list of twenty or thirty cases on each operating day. In 1915 a large number of patients with head wounds were admitted. 'From the surgeons' point of view they were fine cases, for they did well. One lad, who had a bullet removed [...] deep from the brain, was found sitting up sewing at his badge four days afterwards, and greatly pleased with himself. After steel helmets these head injuries decreased in number ...[19]

There were many patients with compound fractures of the femur – 174 at one point in 1917.

The hospital, which was founded only because of strong backing from Sir Alfred Keogh, treated 50,000 patients on its seventeen wards in Holborn Central London. The hospital was also the first to use a new method for bandaging (BIPP), which meant less frequent changes of dressing. Before this wounds were dressed twice a day or even every four hours, with great pain to patients and pressure on staff time. At the end of the war 'The Military Hospital Endell Street became a wonderful and cherished memory.'

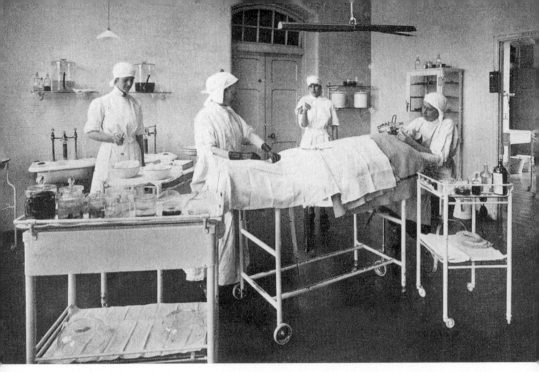

Endell Street was the first surgical hospital (possibly in the world) managed entirely by women doctors.

Eastbourne, Sussex

It was here that the first convalescent hospital was opened in 1915 with 3,840 beds. These were in huts on the western side of the town, underneath the cliffs near Beachy Head. Eastbourne became a specialised centre for the Almeric Paget Massage Corps, a physiotherapy

Hub for rehabilitation: the camp lines at Eastbourne looking towards East Dean Road.

service, and the centres enjoyed the patronage of the Duke of Devon-shire, who owned much of the town. This set the standard as the first of ten military convalescent hospitals, which were assisted by twenty command depots for final stages of rehabilitation:

> The medical treatment in these Command depots was that of graduated exercises, including massage and therapeutic gymnastics, the ultimate object being to harden invalids sufficiently to enable them to join their reserve battalions within six months in a condition for drafting overseas. There we many support staff including the novelty of young working class ambulance drivers.[20]

Oswestry, Shropshire

This was the leading centre for a new network of orthopaedic centres, with 18,540 special beds (with 21,000 staff) compared to 500 beds in 1914.[21] The pioneer, Sir Robert Jones, was the nephew of Hugh Owen Thomas, inventor of the 'Thomas splint' (for stabilising fractures of the femur), which was much used in the First World War. Sir Robert was appointed a Major General in charge of orthopaedics and drove the expansion of the service. From 1917 he was helped by the arrival of American orthopaedic surgeons.

In the last two years of the war there were 317,000 beds in the UK for military patients (compared to 30,000 in 1914) and many of them were specialised for orthopaedics, shell shock, venereal disease and for prisoners of war. The Oswestry centre was a beacon of change in hospital medicine. The Robert Jones and Agnes Hunt Centre in Oswestry is still the leading UK centre for orthopaedics.

Southampton, Hampshire

This was where No. 48 Company of the RAMC, 'in addition to performing clerical and bearer duties at the reception, supplied detachments on the ambulance trains and replaced casualties in hospital ships'.[22] This company also managed the arrival of patients at Dover. During the war 59,710 officers and 1,257,928 other ranks passed through Southampton and 1.3 million through Dover. Distribution of patients to different regions and special hospitals was complex. By 1918 there were twenty ambulance trains carrying more than 8,000 people a day; ambulance trains became a familiar site on main rail lines

Bird's-eye view of St Mark's Hospital.

From stately home to convalescent home, Hatton Grange, Shifnal, Shropshire.

and at major stations. Secondary haemorrhage was the main threat but there were only six deaths out of 2.6 million patients transported on the trains.

Birmingham, Warwickshire

This was regarded as a main centre for Voluntary Aid Detachment staff.[23] This had been set up as part of the Territorial Army in 1910 and the auxiliary nurses played a massive role in the war, both in hospitals and in helping with the transfer of patients and, as in Birmingham, assisting the district nurses:

> The fame of the Birmingham Rest Station has spread far and wide [...] Looking out from the carriage window, the patients in the train see, on the platform, two files of nursing members standing in front of big lorries upon which are set tea urns, mugs, sandwiches, cakes and fruit. There is a shrill whistle and orderlies appear at one in each ward of the trains bearing trays filled with mugs of tea, whilst behind them come the nurses with food and fruit. A little later, cigarettes, pipes and, tobacco and postcards are brought round.[24]

On the way to Birmingham from Southampton there was a canteen on the station in Banbury, which was manned by volunteers for eighteen hours a day for the whole war period. The VAD was one among a number of voluntary movements, including the Red Cross and St John's Ambulance, which gave thousands of hours of unpaid service.

Ministry of National Service, Whitehall, London

In 1920 the Ministry published the results of physical examinations of 2.4 million men by National Service Medical Boards, a unique record up to this time:

> Of ... men of military age (36 per cent) were fit and healthy (22 per cent) were upon a definitely infirm plane of health and strength (30 per cent) were incapable of undergoing more than a very moderate degree of physical exertion and could almost be described with justice as being physical wrecks; and the remaining man was a chronic invalid with a precarious hold on life.[25]

SPECIMENS OF MEN IN EACH OF THE FOUR GRADES.

GRADE I. GRADE II. GRADE III. GRADE IV.

The Ministry of National Service report on 2.4 million medical examinations. By the final two years only 36 per cent were fully fit.

There were, however, great local differences: 30 per cent of men from the cotton industry were graded A, compared to 70 per cent of Welsh anthracite miners. One of the healthiest groups were the 'clerks' of Kingston on Thames.

Craiglockhart, Scotland

This was where war poets Siegfried Sassoon and Wilfred Owen were treated – the place is far more famous now than it was at the time.[26] Most men with shell-shock were treated with short therapy at units in France. The Sassoon/Owen experience is extraordinarily well documented, but also untypical in the extraordinary freedom they were allowed and the sympathetic relationships with psychiatrists.

Beyond shell-shock there was a more general problem of falling motivation and morale. Many years afterwards a battalion RMO (later Churchill's doctor), Dr Charles Wilson (later Lord Moran), advanced the view that courage was a finite resource or 'stock' – most men could only take so much before nerves started to go. This fall in motivation and rise in stress was a more common affliction by 1918. The British Army tried to offset it, with some success, by frequent rotations out of the line and concert parties – by 1918 every division had a full-time troupe of entertainers. The censors found that morale, as reflected in letters home, greatly improved after these events. The efficiency of the postal service – even delivering letters from home to shell holes in the 1918 retreat – also helped, as did the quality and availability of food.

The London Hospital, Whitechapel

It was here that Bertrand Dawson (later Lord Dawson) worked. As a temporary major general on the Western Front he helped organise the medical services and his experience there led him to advocate integration of care between the GP and hospital medicine. His model, as set out in *The Lancet* and in the later Dawson Report, has remained the pioneering statement of what is still the unachieved aim for health services in the UK.[27]

Notes

1 Bosanquet, N., 'Health Systems in Khaki: The British and American Medical Experience' in Cecil, H. and Liddle, P. (eds), *Facing Armageddon*, Pen and Sword, 1996, pp. 451–65.
2 Haldane, R.B., *An Autobiography*, Hodder and Stoughton, 1929, pp. 197–8.
3 Hay, I., *One Hundred Years of Army Nursing*, Cassell, 1953, pp. 89–90.

4 Mitchell, T.J. and Smith, G.M., *Casualties and Medical Statistics*, HMSO, 1931, p. 19.

5 Bosanquet, N., 'Lieutenant General A. Sloggett', *DNB*.

6 Brown, K., *Penicillin Man: Alexander Fleming and the Antibiotic Revolution*, Sutton, 2004, p. 56.

7 Peacock, A.D., 'The Louse Problem at the Western Front', *Journal Royal Army Medical Corps*, Vol. XXVII, pp. 31–60. Byam, W., *Trench Fever: A Louse-Borne Disease*, London, Henry Froude, 1919.

8 Macpherson, W.G., et al., *Medical Services Hygiene of the War*, London, HMSO, 1923, p. 52.

9 Dunn, J.C., *The War the Infantry Knew 1914–19: A Chronicle of Service in France and Belgium*, Jane's, 1967.

10 Chapin, W.A.R., *The Lost Legion*, Springfield, Mass., 1926.

11 Hutchinson, W., *The Doctor in War*, Cassell, 1919, p. 3.

12 Evidence of Colonel J.F.C. Fuller in 'Report of the War Office Committee of Enquiry into "Shell Shock"', HMSO, Cmd 1734, 1922, p. 28.

13 Macpherson, W.G., *Medical Services General History*, Vol. 1, HMSO, 1921, p. 120.

14 *The Times History of the War*, 'The Medical Service of the Royal Navy', Vol. IX, Ch. CXLIV, Printing House Square, 1916, pp. 241–80.

15 Robinson, D.H., *The Dangerous Sky: A History of Aviation Medicine*, G.T. Foulis, 1973, pp. 72–107.

16 Crile, G., *An Autobiography*, Philadelphia Lippincott, 1947, p. 258.

17 Butler, A.G., *Official History of the Australian Medical Services*, Vol. II, 'The Western Front', Australian War Memorial, 1940.

18 Westman, S., *Surgeon with the Kaiser's Army*, William Kimber, 1968, pp. 159–60.

19 Murray, F., *Women as Army Surgeons*, Hodder and Stoughton, 1920.

20 Elliston, R.A., *Eastbourne's Great War 1914–1918*, SB Publications, 1999.

21 Macpherson, W.G., et al., *Medical Services Surgery of the War*, HMSO, 1922, Vol. II pp. 381–459.

22 Chapman-Huston, D. and Rutter, O., *General Sir John Cowans*, Vol. 2, 1924.

23 Bowser, T., *The Story of British V.A.D. Work in the Great War*, Melrose, 1917, pp. 54–67.

24 Sandford, *History of Birmingham in the Great War*.

25 Ministry of National Service, 1917–19, Report, Vol. 1, Physical Examination of Men of Military Age by National Service Medical Boards, 1917–18.

26 Egremont, M., *Siegfried Sassoon: A Biography*, Picador, 2005.

27 Dawson, B., 'The Future of the Medical Profession', *The Lancet*, 20 July 1918, pp. 83–7.

9

Intelligence and Propaganda

The Empires of the future are the Empires of the mind. (Winston Churchill, 1944)

The main intelligence activities were code-breaking and collating information from agents; the Secret Service countering the enemy's spies; the use of camouflage and special effects to mislead the enemy; and the use of information to strengthen morale and win favourable opinion and decisions by other governments. The most developed and best known intelligence gathering was from the war at sea. The Royal Navy developed an intelligence centre, 'Room 40', which scored a vital success in cracking the German Naval Code.[1] They were able to monitor naval messages throughout the war.

Army intelligence had to rely on more miscellaneous sources such as captured documents, prisoner interrogation, aerial reconnaissance, the non-English press and sometimes listening posts on phone lines. Western Front Intelligence also used reports from agent networks within occupied France, Belgium and, notably, Luxembourg, which gave vital information about the movement of German troop trains. Keeping track of German divisions on the Western Front was an even more complex task than tracking the 100 or so ships and U-boats that made up the German naval effort in the North Sea. However, even the most intense and professional intelligence operation could be thrown out by one key variable: the weather. The heavy artillery fire with thousands of shells passing through the atmosphere may have stimulated rainfall, like guns fired at clouds over fruit groves. The weather also affected another key contributor to information – the carrier pigeon, of which there were 20,000 in use on the British front by 1918.[2] The Western

Front intelligence gathering seems to have been separate from that of the navy or even of the War Office and there seems to have been little pooling of information.

Waterloo House, Haymarket, London

The Secret Service had begun as the Secret Service Bureau in a flat in Ashley Gardens, Westminster, in 1909; its main task was to seek out German spies. In 1914 the Bureau had a staff of six. By 1917 its central registry had 27,000 files on suspect individuals and 250,000 cards kept by a staff of 130.[3] It also gathered intelligence by opening letters and telegrams. In January 1916 the secret service became MI5 and by 1918 it had 842 staff based at Waterloo House, 16 Charles Street, Haymarket. Its main work in 1916–18 was to track down subversion by Bolsheviks, Irish nationalists and others. The German spies ceased to be its main workload.

The management of information involved censorship of all letters from the Western Front so that they did not contain any information about personal or unit locations. Standard postcards were on offer with short messages such as 'I am well'. There were also efforts to encourage silence and discretion. At Abbeville station there was a large poster, 'an enormous affair which every warrior on his way to the front must have seen',[4] which ran:

> A wise old owl sat in an oak.
> The more he heard the less he spoke.
> The less he spoke the more he heard.
> Soldiers copy this wise old bird.

Camouflage was a contribution to troop protection and its role grew in importance during the war with the huge increase in artillery. Each battery had to be camouflaged from aerial observation. Here there was cooperation with the French Allies; they lent the word camouflage, devised the techniques and provided the workforce of seamstresses to produce the nets and coloured cloths that were used.

Crewe House, London

This large house in Curzon Street, Piccadilly, is now occupied by the Saudi Arabian Embassy. In 1914 it was owned by the Marquis of

Crewe House: the house of secrets.

Crewe, a member of the Liberal Cabinet, and was lent to the government. It was the main centre for British propaganda throughout the
war. The first task was to influence American opinion, which was
effectively achieved by placing articles in American newspapers via
ghostwriters, one of whom was novelist John Buchan. Later, Crewe
House produced many communications directly to German troops on
the Western Front, even including a poem by Schiller lauding the English. Ludendorff commented on the effectiveness of this propaganda,
as Hitler was to do later in *Mein Kampf*.

   Schiller's poem, 'The Invincible Armada', was picked up by Jünger
and mentioned in his memoirs:[5]

   One look below the Almighty gave
   Where streamed the lion-flags of thy proud foe:
   And near and wider yawned the horrent grave.
   And who, saith He, 'shall lay mine England low –
   The stem that blooms with hero-deeds –
   The rock when man from wrong a refuge needs –

The stronghold where the tyrant comes in vain?
Who shall bid England vanish from the main?
Ne'er this only Eden freedom knew,
Man's stout defence from power to fate consigned.'
God the almighty blew,
And the Armada went to every wind.

At the start of the war there was little appreciation of the need to inform and influence public opinion. War correspondents were banned from the BEF in 1914 and one officer was designated 'eyewitness' to send reports that were created at headquarters rather than in the field. In fact, Colonel Swinton (who had the job) was worthy but not an 'eyewitness' at all. Early on, the power of slogans began to be felt, with Kitchener proving a master of persuasion. One of the earliest successes

One of millions of leaflets dropped on German lines – both sides considered them highly effective.

was the launch of the phrase, 'Old Contemptibles'. In 1954 Major General Hereward Wake, a former intelligence officer, wrote to Leo Amery, who had just published his memoirs:

> On page 21 you say the Kaiser called the British Army 'contemptible'. The true story is this: An intelligence Officer called Bowdler at G.H.Q. (it was some day in September) having nothing better to do invented the army order signed by von Kluck in which occurred the words 'French's contemptible little army'. Some copies of this were typed and distributed at G.H.Q. The copy I got I shoved into a letter I was writing to my father-in-law, Mr Robert Benson—not that I believed it. Judge my astonishment when I saw it in *The Times* a few days later. Mr Benson had taken it straight off to the Editor. At the same time Mr B wrote and asked me for the original German of the order, as he found 'contemptible' a bit difficult and observed that the German soldiers would hardly know French by name – and so on. By that time I judged it best to say – no more. The 'old contemptibles' were out of control.[6]

This was an early success for Lord Northcliffe, the owner of *The Times*, and he followed it up in May 1915 with a press story that brought about the fall of the government; the revelations of shell shortages led Prime Minister Asquith to dismantle the last fully Liberal government and set up a coalition government. There was success, too, in influencing public opinion in the United States via the Bryce report on German atrocities in Belgium. There was also success in putting across the British case on the *Lusitania*. It was in the struggle for American opinion that the vital realisation dawned of the importance of communication and persuasion. The word 'propaganda' appeared in 1918 and summed up certain techniques of mass persuasion using simplified messages and mass distribution through leaflets. The man who brought about the vast expansion was none other than Lord Northcliffe, then assisted by a future press baron, Lord Beaverbrook. Lord Northcliffe was put in charge of all British propaganda based at Crewe House.

Other methods of communication included the coming of the war artists, which were accredited from 1915 onwards. They started with a low-key, realistic approach, as with the drawings of Muirhead Bone, and later became more futurist and abstract, ranging from Wyndham Lewis to Paul Nash. The exhibitions were popular at the time and did not provoke such a level of anguish as the war poets, but the war poets were their own masters (all the government provided for them was possibly a notebook and a pencil, and their writings were not subject to

The Ministry of Information cinemotor. Within six weeks, a third of the population had seen the 'Battle of the Somme' in 1916.

censorship). The pictures, on the whole, presented some desolation but also much strenuous effort and dedication. It was only after the war that the more grim examples, such as John Singer Sargent's 'Gassed', were shown. There were no 'official' war poets and their work was only circulated widely well after the war. On the German side most of the war artists were unofficial (apart from Hindenburg's personal portraitist) and their work was similar in tone to the British war poets.

Broadstairs/Elmwood, Near Sandwich, Kent

John Buchan, while convalescing from a duodenal ulcer in Broadstairs, wrote *The Thirty Nine Steps* in 1914, at a time of spy mania.[7] The '39 steps' were the years of his age at the time and in Broadstairs (Bradgate in the novel) they are the escape route that failed. In fact, the actual steps (near Buchan's boarding house) can be seen from the coast road and there were seventy-eight of them.

Two miles further along the coast there was the country house of Lord Northcliffe. Such was his fearsome repute in Germany that he gained the personal attention of destroyers, which, on July 1916, fired six shells into Elmwood. They succeeded in killing the gardener and the gardener's child but missed the noble Lord.[8] He announced that he would die in bed and refused to take shelter, but later filed a report on

German destroyers bombarded the home of newspaper and publishing magnate Lord Northcliffe in Elmwood, Kent.

the raid to *The Times*. Elmwood is now the clubhouse of a golf course and is visible from the road.

Post Office Headquarters, St Martin's Le Grand, London

The first intelligence success came an hour after the declaration of war. At midnight on 4 August orders went out to the Post Office headquarters in St Martin's Le Grand to cut all German cables to the outside world, and before dawn the cable ship CS *Alert* was on her way from Harwich to grapple them up. By mid-morning the cables had been cut and Germany had no communication with the wider world except through the short-wave wireless station in Nauen, near Berlin. The building in St Martin's Le Grand is still there, behind St Paul's Cathedral, but no longer occupied by the Post Office.

The Post Office of course delivered thousands of letters and parcels and managed the telegram and telephone services, but it also carried

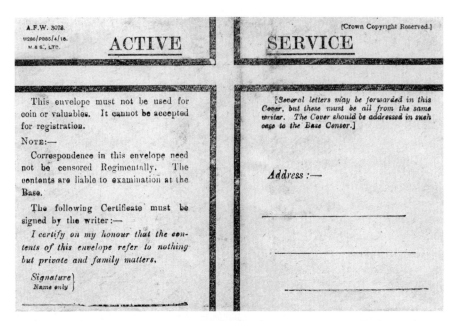

For the Post Office – an Active Service Envelope was only censored at base.

out censorship of all letters, including those in other languages, for which it employed hundreds of bilingual women staff. The Post Office also managed the separation allowances for relatives and the War Savings Bonds, with the Tank Bank as its savings symbol in 1917–18.

For the work of letter and parcel sorting for the troops, the Post Office set up a temporary wooden building covering 5 acres in Regent's Park. Every week, 12.5 million letters left Britain for the Western Front, some 16,000 mail bags per day. Some 2,500 women worked in this office and international letters were sorted in the King's Cross area at Mount Pleasant sorting office. The telegraph service was disrupted for a few days by a Gotha raid on the Central Telegraph Office in July 1917 and Birmingham took over as the central office for three days. No one was hurt, thanks to a national early warning system developed by the Post Office engineering department. In June 1918 the Penny Post, after seventy-five years, had to make way for a 1½p post.

Old Admiralty Building, London

This was the first purpose-built office building in London, dating from 1723, and still stands on the Mall near Trafalgar Square. On the first floor, Room 40 was the main centre for naval intelligence. This room was close to the First Sea Lord's offices and looked out over the closed

Churchill's map case at the Old Admiralty near Room 40.

courtyard at the back. In the course of research for this book we were able to find Churchill's map case in the old Board Room. We were also able to locate the most likely venue for Room 40, which is now used by staff from the Foreign and Commonwealth Office (FCO). It was here that the staff cracked the naval codes dredged up after the cruiser *Magdeburg* had sunk off the Moon Islands in Estonia. The Russian Navy had dredged up the code book and sent it on to the Admiralty. By December 1914 Room 40 was able to follow all signals from the Imperial German Navy. It was in Room 40 that, in January 1917, the staff – led by the Presbyterian minister (and translator of the works of Albert Schweitzer) Reverend William Montgomery and a young publisher, Hugh de Grey – were able to decode the Zimmermann telegram proposing an alliance between Germany, Mexico and Japan to reconquer Texas and California. This message drove the United States into the war only a few months after the president had won re-election on the slogan: 'He kept us out of the War.'[9]

The building is visible from the south side of Admiralty Arch. It is occupied by the FCO and is currently being refurbished, but it is hoped that once this is done some escorted visits might be possible to this room, which should be a World Heritage Site for naval intelligence.

Folkestone, Kent

This was the hub for intelligence concerning troop movements behind the German lines. The network of agents was run from an office at 8 The Parade by Major Cameron. The agents, who included railway workers in Luxembourg, supplied details of German train numbers, which were vital in predicting the numbers transferred from the East in 1918, but also for more routine reports.

The office at 8 The Parade, Folkestone is still there, although in need of repair.[10] The street is a short cul-de-sac leading from Bayle Street. There is no through traffic and the site is secluded. At the end of the street are some steps down to the harbour. There has been little change in the terrace in the last 100 years.

Notes

1 Beesley, P., *Room 40: British Naval Intelligence 1914–18*, Hamish Hamilton, 1982.

2 Priestley, W.J., *Work of the Royal Engineers in the European War, 1914-1919: The Signal Service in the European War, France*, Mackay, 1921, pp. 53–4.

3 Andrew, C,. *The Defence of the Realm: The Authorised History of MI5*, Allen Lane, Penguin, 2009, p. 58.

4 Spears, E., *Prelude to Victory*, Heinemann, 1940.

5 Jünger, E., *The Storm of Steel*, p. 302.

6 Amery, L., *My Political Life*, Vol. 11, Hutchinson, 1953, p. 21.

7 Buchan, J., *Memory Hold the Door*, Hodder and Stoughton, 1940, p. 195.

8 Pound, R. and Harmsworth, G., *Northcliffe*, Cassell, 1959, p. 522.

9 Tuchman, B,. *The Zimmermann Telegram*, 1957. For the full remarkable story of the exploitation by the British of the Zimmerman telegram and the reading of German naval and diplomatic signals, see *Blinker Hall: The Man who Brought America into World War I* by David Ramsay.

10 Morgan, J., *The Secrets of Rue St Roch*, Allen Lane, 2004, p. 42.

10

The Supreme Command: from Muddle to Mission

Towards the end of September the King made another munitions tour ... He picked out one worker at Sheffield, whom he recognised as having served with him when he was a midshipman on HMS *Bacchante*. He watched another making shells and remarked to him: 'I am glad you realise the importance of the work in hand. Without an adequate supply of shells we cannot expect to win'. Words like these uttered 'man to man' by the Head of State to the artisan, naturally ran like wildfire through the works.[1]

The political personalities showed little change from pre-war days, but this was not true of the organisations. Personalities from the late nineteenth century presided over organisations that were to set a model for much of the twentieth, with its central planning and production drives.

Asquith, Lloyd George and Balfour had all been in politics two decades before the war. The only dynamic young leader (Churchill) was discarded by a conspiracy of disloyal colleagues, with two vital years of power lost before his rehabilitation as Minister of Munitions: 'These three men, the politician, the soldier (Kitchener) and the sailor (Fisher), were to figure in an unblessed trinity of mutual destruction.'[2] It was an exclusive club of political leaders with many dim political figures in the second rank. In France, the nation turned to older men – two wartime premiers were over 75, Ribot (81) and Clemenceau (78). The leaders and generals of Imperial Germany were also old. This was a war with the maximum contrast in generations between those who fought and those who ruled. Among wartime leaders in Britain, only Churchill and Kitchener had seen military service.

The Labour ministers were newcomers but, in fact, Arthur Henderson and John Robert Clynes had been in parliament for a long time. Henderson had joined the Labour forces after being rejected as the Liberal candidate for Newcastle as far back as 1895. The real gate-crashers were the press barons led by Lord Northcliffe and Viscount Rothermere. They were feared for their power and for their unpredictability. The fourth estate was a new force in politics that emerged during the war, with Lloyd George as maestro.

The political club presided over a change in organisation mainly engineered from below. In central government, change was driven by the first Cabinet Secretary, Hankey, who had earlier been Secretary of the Committee on Imperial Defence. At the age of 84 in 1961 he published two volumes on the Supreme Command (partly based on diaries), which were an incisive account of government before and during the war.[3]

He presented the war not as a sudden crisis, but the expected culmination of a threat that had been growing over twenty-five years. To meet this there had been much advance planning. He gave credit to the Committee of Imperial Defence, created by Balfour as prime minister in 1905. There had been complete reorganisation of the navy to bring about the concentration of new and powerful forces in the North Sea. The pre-war emphasis had been on sea power as the key British weapon. He gives greater credit to Fisher's reorganisation of the navy than to Haldane's reorganisation of the army, which lacked a clear mission. The size of the BEF was 100,000 and this had been set in 1904 – before the staff talks with France –– as the likely size required for intervention in India against the Russian threat. The size remained unchanged, even when the likely mission had altered fundamentally. However, there was an advance plan, or 'War Book', with telegrams drafted ready to send to every part of government.

The first year of the war was marked by administrative confusion, with a cabinet that did not issue any minutes or records of its decisions:

> With no regular, systematised contact between statesmen, sailors and soldiers, with no War Council or War Committee devoting itself exclusively to the central problems of the war as a whole, with no inter-allied Council and with no cabinet secretariat there was no one responsible for anticipating events and working out plans for dealing with the various emergencies that might arise.[4]

The result, as with Antwerp and Kitchener's decisions on the New Army and also on Gallipoli, was a 'tendency for a small group of Ministers to take emergency decisions without summoning the full cabinet'.[5]

The First Imperial War Cabinet.

From 1917 there was a small war cabinet of five members, with a larger imperial war cabinet backed up by a secretariat. This included outside experts housed in the garden suburb – the Gardens of Downing Street – together with temporary buildings in the lake, which was drained in St James Park. This new system was effective under Lloyd George's leadership. It amounted to an 'elective dictatorship', which developed rapid and effective solutions such as the convoys, the setting up of the RAF, the propaganda war, the definition of war aims and managing the aftershock from the Russian Revolutions. Rapid decision-making and a sense of common purpose, in which aims were related to the resources available, replaced the free-range activities of the early part of the war. Lloyd George also made a great effort to communicate with the public. His management of the home front opinion later drew admiration both from Lenin and from Hitler in *Mein Kampf*. Government became much more public and much less contained in secret committees in Whitehall.

10 Downing Street, London

This address was little known before 1914 but during the war became a familiar seat of power. Two prime ministers (Asquith 1908–16 and then Lloyd George 1916–22) occupied it during the war. Under Lloyd George it became a social hub, especially for working breakfasts, as well as a business centre, however, it did not gain its later role as the setting for state dinners, as Lloyd George preferred to be in bed by 9 p.m. and held evening meetings very rarely. Churchill credited him with:

> ... the seeing eye, that deep original instinct which peers through the surfaces of words and things [...] Against this industry, learning, scholarship, eloquence, social influence, wealth, reputation, and orderly mind, plenty of pluck counted for little or nothing.[6]

Lloyd George set a record for the longest continuous stay in Downing Street since Walpole (fourteen years), first as chancellor then as prime minister. It remained open until barriers had to be placed against possible IRA attacks in 1920. By 1920 the titles of such volumes as *Mirrors of Downing Street* needed no further explanation.[7]

The Wharf, Sutton Courtenay, Oxfordshire

This was the weekend retreat of the Asquiths. Photographs of Asquith relaxing with members of the artistic Bloomsbury group were only published much later, but his reputation for over-long weekends (with departures from Downing Street at 3 p.m. on Friday) was current, and contributed to the decline of his political reputation, until the plaintive cry of Margot Asquith, in her diary for June 1916, 'We are out; it can only be a question of time now when we shall leave Downing Street.'[8] After ten confused years in opposition he died as Earl of Oxford in this house. This is still a private dwelling, although fronting onto a public road in the village.

Walton Heath, Surrey

This was Lloyd George's usual weekend retreat, except on the rare occasions he went to Churt in North Wales. The house had survived a bomb attack by suffragettes in 1911. Lloyd George was able to play golf at the Walton Heath golf club, specially developed by the Liberal peer and proprietor of the *News of the World*, Lord Riddell. The site today is a private dwelling although discreetly visible from the road in Walton Heath. The distinctly exclusive golf club is still there.

2 Carlton House Terrace, London

It was here that Kitchener lived for most of his time at the War Office. Sometimes, on a Saturday morning, he went down to his recently acquired estate, Broome Park, near Folkestone in Kent (now a hotel), to preside over his collection of rare oriental porcelains and supervise works of renovation. He would return on Sunday evening.

Whitehall, London

The term came into common use during the First World War, reflecting the vast expansion of offices that took over every building and hotel in the area. This was, and is, one of the widest roads in London and viewed from Trafalgar Square towards the Houses of Parliament it has a slight kink in the middle where the old palace gatehouse was. The whole of the supreme command and its supporting agencies were located in a few hundred metres of space in and around Whitehall.

The buildings are monumental, steeling occupants to national resolve. They were like a volcano erupting with the lava of control. The

Whitehall.

Lloyd George with Haig and Marshal Joseph Joffre; the frocks and the brass hats. 'Were these glittering commands to be entrusted to mediocrities, bred with obsolete tactics, and mouldering in military routine?'

orders from these buildings, once on the march, could not be stopped and were a compelling force reaching down into the lives of thousands of individuals. Even a prime minister could not stop them, as Lloyd George found out when he tried to halt the Passchendaele offensive in 1917. The volcanoes are now extinct but the power can still be sensed in the canyons of Whitehall Place. These buildings were the pillars of world domination.

Hotel Metropole, Northumberland Avenue, London

The Ministry of Munitions started in 6 Whitehall Gardens. The name Whitehall Gardens has now shifted to the Embankment and its former row of houses has been demolished. From June 1915 Whitehall Gardens housed the cabinet secretariat and the new Ministry of Munitions, as well as the Committee of Imperial Defence. In late 1915 the Ministry of Munitions moved to the Hotel Metropole in Northumberland Avenue. This is a large building, which has been refurbished as the Hotel Corinthia. The stone letters 'MH' (Metropole Hotel) are visible above the Northumberland Avenue entrance.

41 Cromwell Road, London

It was here that Churchill lived during the war, moving in 1918 to Sussex Gardens on the 'wrong side of the park'. His memoirs, *The World Crisis*, were written later as the first literary effort of many at Chartwell in Kent. From Churchill came the original and authoritative condemnation of the 1917 Passchendaele offensive:

> It cannot be said that the soldiers, that is to say the Staff, did not have their way. They tried their sombre experiment to its conclusion. They took all they required from Britain. They wore down alike the manhood and guns of the British Army almost to destruction. They did it in face of the plainest warnings and of arguments which they could not answer.[9]

Churchill particularly stressed the loss of experienced officers 'out of all proportion to the great losses of the rank and file' – more than 5,000 had been killed outright and over 15,000 had been wounded in the Passchendaele offensive. This loss 'could never in fact be replaced'.[10]

He recorded how at the time:

> Mr Lloyd George viewed with horror the task imposed on him of
> driving to the shambles by stern laws the remaining manhood of the
> nation. Lads of eighteen and nineteen, elderly men up to forty-five, the
> last surviving brother, the only son of his mother (and she a widow),
> the father the sole support of the family, the weak, the consumptive,
> the thrice wounded – all must now prepare themselves for the scythe.[11]

Australia House, London

This was finished during the war as a symbol of the new Australia. The
nineteenth-century policy of self-governing Dominions proved a huge
success in mobilising support. The Australian prime minister, Billy
Hughes, spent most of 1918 in the United Kingdom. Lloyd George
even included in the war cabinet a permanent empire representative, in
the person of South African leader, General Smuts.

The Houses of Parliament, London

Like the French Assemblée Nationale, the UK parliament remained
surprisingly free and active during the war – but the activities were
very different. The French assembly played a key role in the rise and
fall of governments (five during the war) and also in monitoring the
war effort.

The UK parliament played very little part in monitoring the war
effort and none at all in the rise and fall of governments (three during
the war period). Lloyd George, as prime minister, rarely came to parliament and delegated the duty to his chancellor, Bonar Law, a Liberal prime minister supported mainly by Conservatives. In 1918–19,
during the peace negotiations, he did not attend parliament at all.
The great set-piece parliamentary challenge in the Maurice Debate of
April 1918 (about whether Lloyd George had blocked reinforcements
to the Western Front) led to the total triumph of the executive. Most
of Lloyd George's major speeches, such as his speech on war aims in
January 1918, which greatly influenced the 'fourteen points' of President Wilson, were made to audiences outside parliament – in that case
to the Trades Union Congress.

The Commons did play an important role as a safety valve for dis-
content and in representing causes. Sir Frederick Markham was a

persistent advocate for under-age soldiers and Pemberton Billing, the Member for Air, forced the transfer of squadrons from the Western Front to combat air raids. In parliament this was the hour of the populist. Outsize personalities emerged but not as in the Second World War alternative parties such as the Commonwealth Party. Parliament was also a forum for giving a hearing to unpopular causes, such as the small group of anti-war MPs led by Ramsey MacDonald and later Lord Lansdowne, with his case for a negotiated peace to stop 'the slaughter of the nation's best manhood'.

The war did promote a new consensus on the need for a wider franchise, so that in 1918 Britain moved closer to universal suffrage, with votes for all men over 21 and women over 30. Younger women got the vote in the 1920s.

Buckingham Palace, London

For Queen Victoria the people were cleared from the pavements as she drove though cities; Edward VII waved to the people but kept them at a distance. It was George V who began to meet the people on tours with a gruelling programme, which took him to every industrial area and some many times over. His personal commitment included a pledge of abstinence and, unlike the Kaiser who continued with the full range of pre-war delicacies, the King and Queen had ration books. The King, as a former naval officer, also visited naval ships, including the dreadnought squadron commanded by Admiral Rodman. Queen Mary was active in visiting hospitals and convalescent homes.

The King directed that potatoes, cabbages and other vegetables should replace geraniums in the flowerbeds surrounding the Queen Victoria Memorial outside Buckingham Palace and in the Royal Parks. George V personally signed letters to returning prisoners – about 150,000 of them – and in 1918 he also sent a letter to every American soldier landing in the UK.

Perhaps the most poignant moment affirming the new relationship between the King and his people was his call for united prayer – a day of intercession – on 6 January, the first Sunday of 1918:

I therefore hereby appoint January 6th – the first Sunday of the year – to be set aside as a special day of prayer and thanksgiving in all the churches throughout my dominions and require that this proclamation be read at the services held on that day.

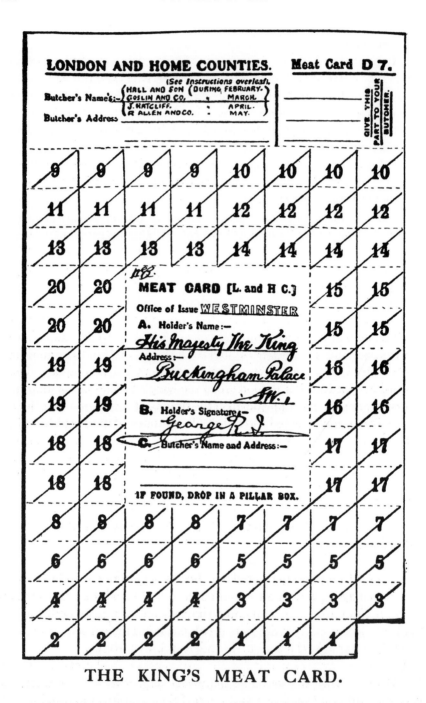

THE KING'S MEAT CARD.

The King's meat ration card. Unlike the Kaiser, the King and Queen had ration books.

To My People

The world-wide struggle for the triumph of right and liberty is entering upon its last and most difficult phase. The enemy is striving by desperate assault and subtle intrigue, to perpetuate the wrongs already committed and stem the tide of a free civilisation. We have yet to complete the great task to which more than three years ago, we dedicated ourselves.

At such a time I would call upon you to devote a special day to prayer that we may have the clear-sightedness and strength necessary to the victory of our cause ...[12]

Across the empire, from a summer day in Otago in the South Island of New Zealand to the winter haze of Leeds in the UK and on to Vancouver in Canada, the churches were packed and overflowing for the reading of the message and the service of prayer:

In Leeds on the first Sunday afternoon in January, there was a most moving and memorable service held in the Town Hall where a representative gathering occupied every seat and yard of standing room, and even overflowed on to the steps in Victoria Square. The Lord Mayor (Mr Frank Gott) read the King's Proclamation and the vast concourse of people joined in the singing of the National Anthem [...] The organ boomed forth the solemn tones of the Dead March; the Last Post was sounded; and with thrilling effect the congregation hymned their intercessions for Divine protection for the sailors, soldiers, sick and wounded and anxious ones at home.[13]

The Bank of England, Threadneedle Street, London

The Bank of England marketed war bonds very actively and was effective in managing war finance, but could not conceal the vast overhang of debt. There were special campaigns aimed at school children and 'tank weeks' in many cities with 'tank banks'. The last remaining tank from these tank weeks is to be found in Ashford, Kent.

The bank was assisted by the government's American agent, J.P. Morgan, who showed a keen stewardship of British interests, and was also aided by the great success of Liberty Bonds in allowing continued dollar loans to Britain. For this, Britain had to pay in gold under shotgun guard.

Shotguns in hand, men unload and
check the arrival of £10 million worth
of English gold in New York.

Who Won the War?

The central problem in Whitehall for the last two years of the war was
the friction between the civilian and military leaders – the frocks and
the brass hats. The conflict raged throughout 1917. The first success
of the ministers was in changing the leadership of the navy – removing
Jellicoe as First Sea Lord and installing Geddes as minister. The intran-
sigent Robertson (who wrote in a private letter 'The Prime Minister

Applying for the war loan in the Bank of England courtyard.

Children buying the war loan with their own pence saved.

is an underbred swine'[14]) went in February 1918 and Haig's powers were curtailed by introducing Foch as supreme commander. The bitterness remained intense and came to a head with the Maurice Debate on 9 May 1918, concerning whether Lloyd George had blocked reinforcements from the Western Front. In his life of Churchill, Roy Jenkins pointed out the unusual bitterness of Lloyd George's index entry in his war memoirs on Maurice some fifteen years later.[15]

However, the wise Hankey rated the new supreme command a success. Driving from Folkestone on 6 November:

> Throughout that long and lonely night without headlights, for we were still under war conditions, I pondered over the events of the last four years. I saw in my mind a panorama of all that long sequence – the weary years of failure and defeat; the many frustrated hopes; the dramatic change in August 1918; the delirium of victory. What had brought it about? What nation and what individual had made the greatest contribution / what were the fundamental causes? Who was the man who won the war? So, as the storm swept car drew in at the gates of my modest country home (in Oxshott) and roused a household anxious at my non-arrival, I said to myself – LLOYD GEORGE WAS THE MAN WHO WON THE WAR.[16]

There was a magnetic pull of people – and money – towards London. By the end of the war, 70 per cent of GDP was being funnelled through Whitehall. But there was a contrast between the vast administrative machine in the background and the war of small teams, crews and platoons – their courage and drive were there day in and day out. It was a long war and all depended on the initiative of these small groups. In the Second World War Churchill was to reflect after the fall of Tobruk in 1942: 'They did not fight like their fathers.'

The war was a challenge to a generation – a challenge met with great courage and energy. The threat was tangible. In Britain the guns could be heard some way inland and in France, as Churchill reported in 1918, 'From the heights of Montmartre the horizon could be seen alive with the flashes of artillery.' The war the generals got was not the one they wanted.

For individuals the war brought changed personal experience and personal strain. Almost every family was touched by loss of close relatives or friends, yet for many there was also opportunity and further training. The Armistice came suddenly with a huge sense of relief. Churchill wrote that at the chime of eleven o'clock:

Men and women came scurrying into the street. The bells of London began to clash. Northumberland Avenue was now crowded with people in hundreds, nay thousands, rousing hither and thither in a frantic manner shouting and screaming with joy. The tumult grew. It grew like a gale, but from all sides simultaneously. The street was now a seething mass of humanity. Flags appeared as if by magic. Streams of men and women flowed from the Embankment. They mingled with torrents pouring down the Strand on their way to acclaim the King. Almost before the last stroke of the clock had died away, the strict, war rationed regulated streets of London had become a triumphant pandemonium [...] Safety, freedom, peace, home the dear one back at the fireside – all after fifty-two months of gaunt distortion.[17]

Later that evening, fires were lit at the foot of Nelson's Column. The scorch marks were kept for twenty years and there are still some faint signs today on the lion to the north-west.

There was a legacy of political insecurity: Britain had a vastly expanded empire in Africa and the Middle East without the means to defend it. There was also an industrial legacy: the new, more technical, businesses that grew out of the war were the basis for a strong recovery in the 1930s and for improvements in living standards and health, which have been masked by the era of the Great Depression. Geddes was one leader in the development of Fort Dunlop in Birmingham[18] and Tesco grew out of a business selling post-war surplus stores in Well Street market in 1919.

For twenty-five years after the First World War Britain was, for the only time in the twentieth century, the world leader in innovation, with the jet engine, radar, television and penicillin all descended from First World War activities. The jet engine was mainly sponsored by the RAF; radar developed from First World War experiments with sound detection using concrete structures to detect sound waves; television grew out of experiments in image transmission; and penicillin was the last development of the Wright-Fleming team, who had been leaders in RAMC pathology. Even as late as the 1950s, Bragg was the leader in funding research that led to the discovery of DNA.[19]

Much of the British war effort was well organised. For many in government the war was not a surprise, but for the people of Britain it was. It brought massive new commitments and great sacrifice. We can be proud of how this generation of people in Britain faced this test.

The First World War was a victory over the German military forces brought about by mobilisation of assets built up in the nineteenth century, the political success of Dominion status in creating a sense of loyalty, and the economic success of local entrepreneurs and skilled workers, many in small centres in the Midlands and the East of England. It was also a success for the voluntary spirit, as well as for government organisation – from the New Army, through the role of the thousands of VADs, and of Boy Scouts.

The exhilaration of victory was short-lived. The war and its aftermath released dark forces and created a political space that was to be filled by evil. There was no Pax Britannica to bring about a century of peace, as had happened after 1815. The military victory was soon lost in the political maelstrom of the next thirty years. As the great French historian Élie Halévy said in a lecture in Oxford in 1929, war and revolution came together.[20] The end of one war was followed by revolutions, which in turn brought about more wars. The Armistice turned out to be a truce, not a peace settlement.

Notes

1 Lloyd George, D., *War Memoirs*, Vol. 1, p. 321.
2 Hough, R., *Former Naval Person: Churchill and the War at Sea*, Weidenfeld and Nicolson, p. 23.
3 Hankey, Lord, *The Supreme Command 1914–1918*, George Allen and Unwin, 1961.
4 Ibid, p. 178.
5 Ibid, p. 198.
6 Churchill, W.S., *Great Contemporaries*, 1943, Macmillan, p. 212. This volume covers many figures but has one strange omission – Lloyd George. This passage is taken from the essay on Curzon.
7 A Gentleman with a Duster, *The Mirrors of Downing Street*, Mills and Boon, 1920.
8 Grigg, J., *Lloyd George From Peace to War 1912–16*, Methuen, 1985, p. 361.
9 Churchill, W.S., *The World Crisis 1916–18*, Part II, Thornton Butterworth, 1927, p. 339.
10 Ibid, p. 375.
11 Ibid, p. 377.
12 Williamson, P., *National Days of Prayer: The Churches, The State and Public Worship in Britain 1899–1957*, English Heritage website review, 14 February 2013.
13 Scott, W.H., op. cit. pp. 58–9.
14 Woodward, D.R. (ed), *The Military Correspondence of Field Marshal Sir William Robertson*, Army Record Society, p. 213. Letter 9 August 1917 to Lt General Sir L.E. Kiggell.
15 Lloyd George, *War Memoirs*, Vol. xi, p.3,496.
16 Hankey, op. cit., p. 872.
17 Churchill, W.S., op. cit., pp. 542–3.
18 Greaves, K., op. cit., pp. 108–33.
19 Hunter, G.K., *Light is Messenger: The Life and Science of William Lawrence Bragg*, OUP, 2004, pp. 195–6.
20 Halévy, É., *The World Crisis of 1914–18, An Interpretation*, Oxford, 1930.

Postscript

The British People at War

Examining the casualty list.

Cheerful recruits entering a London railway station.

Some good advice in Piccadilly.

[By special permission of the proprietors of "Punch."

" OH, MOTHER, I *DO* THINK IT UNFAIR ABOUT THE ZELLEPIN! EVERYBODY
SAW IT BUT ME. *WHY* DIDN'T YOU WAKE ME?"
"NEVER MIND, DARLING, YOU SHALL SEE IT NEXT TIME—IF YOU'RE VERY
GOOD."

A child's view of a Zeppelin from *Punch* magazine.

Passengers handling their own luggage.

A new use for Lords cricket ground; geese in their compound.

A Glasgow crowd waiting to buy whisky.

Munitions workers at dinner at the Greyhound State Tavern.

An economy poster.

SACRIFICE LUXURY FOR VICTORY

A New Hat	Will buy	4 Steel Helmets
A New Dress		4 Service Rifles
A Fur Coat		A Machine Gun
A Diamond Tiara		A Field Gun
A Bottle of Champagne		100 Cartridges
A Box of Cigars		400 do
A Lap Dog		20 Shells
A Piano		100 do.
A Motor Car		An Aeroplane

**OLD ENGLAND. FIRST
SELF. SECOND**

A crowd waiting patiently in line to purchase potatoes.

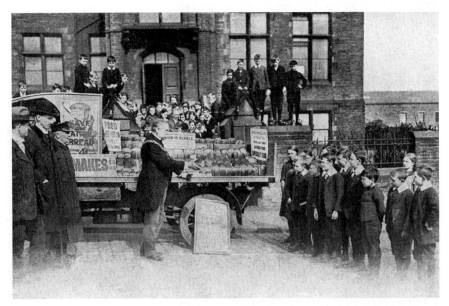

A lesson on food economy by the Mayor of Keighley.

Messengers and Australian soldiers at the Bank of England obtaining war loan prospectuses.

Digging allotments along the side of a railway.

School children taking home coal in their dinner hour.

Ransacking a German baker's shop in Caledonian Road after an air raid on London.

Well to-do people taking home their own coal.

A woman bargee.

Signing the registration form at a City hotel – a new requirement in the war.

The Land at War

Middlesbrough

Horseferry Road & Park Royal

Sandhurst

Aldershot

Chatham

Shirehampton

Salisbury Plain

Folkestone & Hythe

Chattri on the Downs

Army, Allies and Memorials

Newcastle
Birtley
Gretna
Leeds
Liverpool
Firth, Sheffield
Queensferry
Chilwell
Birmingham
Enfield Lock   Woolwich, Arsenal
Vickers, Crayford   Shoeburyness

Munitions

Logistics

New Weapons

War at Sea

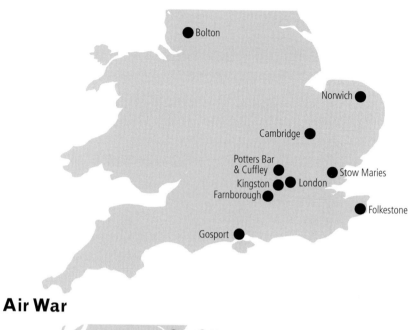

Air War

Medical Services

Intelligence and Propaganda

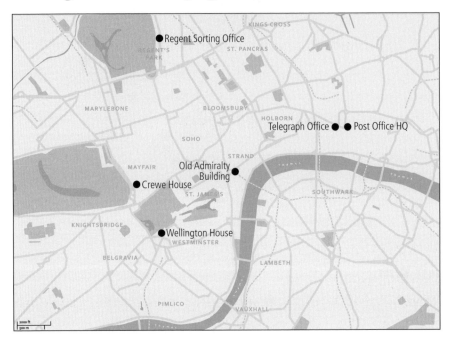

The Supreme Command

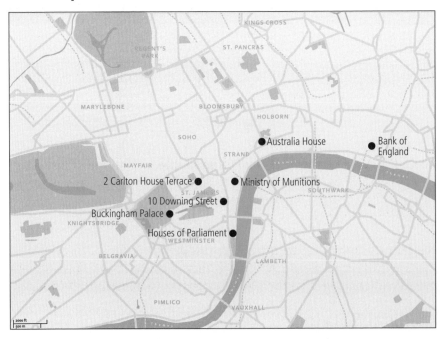

Guide

Chapter 2

The War Office
Whitehall (**SW1A 2HB**) is located between Whitehall Place and Horse Guards Avenue.

Aldershot
From the M3 take the A331. The best approach is from the north via Queen's Avenue. Follow the signs to the museum (**GU11 2LG**), which is excellent.

Salisbury Plain
From London, on the A303, take the A3028 to Bulford and Larkhill. The first airstrip is in Larkhill – left into Hills Road. The original hangar is at the end of the road on the left.

Grantham
From the A1 take the A607 to Belton House, a National Trust property (**NG32 2LS**). MGC huts were to the south of the house on the slopes, which have since been built on. The park has a perimeter road with the Machine Gun Memorial near the South Gate.

Royal Engineers, Chatham
The museum is in the former Royal Engineers Barracks. Take the A2 to Gillingham/Chatham then follow signs to the museum (**ME4 4UG**).

Chapter 3

Folkestone
M20 from London, exit 12. Left to Shorncliffe St Martin's Plain. Main Canadian camp. Follow the signs to the Leas and the Road of Remembrance down to the port at the eastern end. The Intelligence HQ is at 8 The Parade (**CT20 1SN**) – a continuation of Bayle Street (not the Marine Parade).

Codford
On A36 between Salisbury and Warminster. Take the road into the village. The ANZAC graves are in the churchyard and the NZ Hospital was in a ravine to the north of the village. Sutton Veny is 3 miles further on the left, past Heytesbury (home of Siegfried Sassoon). The Great War buildings are part of an industrial estate to the west of the village. The graves in the churchyard include those of a young (15+) Australian.

Liverpool Stanley Park
The Elm House Pub (with baseball photos) is in Townsend Lane (**L4 4LZ**). Stanley Park, where the baseball was played, is north of Priory Road (**L4 2SL**).

Brighton, The Chattri
Take the A23 from London and then take the roundabout to the A27 towards Lewes. The footpath to the Chattri (**BN1 8ZB**) is well marked.

Chapter 4

Woolwich Arsenal
DLR (soon Crossrail) to Woolwich Arsenal. By the main gate in Beresford Street take No. 1 Street to Firepower – an interesting Royal Artillery museum (**SE18 6ST**). There are a few First World War buildings on the left – the main conversions have been of eighteenth- and nineteenth-century buildings. Note the pier for shipping of guns for testing at Shoeburyness in Essex on the extreme eastern point of the Thames Estuary.

Gretna
From the M6, take exit 22 to the A75 (beware of speed cameras). The main First World War buildings are at Eastrigg – Unwin's planned town. From April to October you can visit the The Devil's Porridge museum (**DG12 6TQ**).

Chilwell

Exit 25 from M1. A52 towards Nottingham then right onto the B6003 and left on the A6005. Site is Chetwynd Barracks (**NG9 5HA**), named after the founder of the First World War filling plant, and is still used by the MoD. There is a memorial inside the camp and also one to the 129 killed in July 1918, buried in a shared grave in Attenborough churchyard (when last visited, the memorial was badly in need of renovation).

Leeds, Barnbow/Crossgates

M1, exit 46 to Crossgates. The memorial is in the middle of the roundabout in the centre of Crossgates. The site of the plant is in Manston Lane (**LS15 8HZ**).

Liverpool, Cunard Works, Rimrose Road

L20. Bootle Corner of Rimrose Road and Peel Road.

Enfield Lock

The site of the Royal Small Arms factory is off the A1055, Mollison Avenue. There is a small museum in the Enfield Island housing development (**EN3**). Further north is the Waltham Abbey Powder Works, managed by a charity with a number of First World War buildings.

Vickers, Crayford

Site is in Crayford Road. The entrance buildings are still there, as is the canteen building, which was later used as a town hall.

Sheffield

M1, exit 34 off the Sheffield–Rotherham road, Firth/Hadfield site is at Tinsley, with some First World War buildings on a large industrial site (**S9 1**).

Chapter 5

Willesden Junction

Station approach off Old Oak lane (**NW10 4UY**). Good view from High level Station. The largest marshalling yard was at Old Oak Common to the south.

Newhaven

Off the A26. First World War yards were to the left, before the harbour. There is a small museum well worth visiting (**BN9 0DH**).

Folkestone
Troops de-trained at Shorncliffe Station, now West Folkestone (**CT20 3PA**), and marched along the Leas to the Road of Remembrance down to the harbour. VIPs came directly to the pier by train. The rail embankment to Folkestone Dock is still there.

Dover
There is a fine view of the harbour from West Cliff, off the A20.

Richborough
Mystery port was on the banks of the River Stour, off the A256 towards Pegwell Bay.

Basingstoke
Follow the signs to Milestones museum (**RG22 6PG**), exit on M3. Well worth visiting for its display on Thornycroft Lorries. The site of the plant is now a Morrisons supermarket. The entrance sign for the supermarket is propped on the remains of a crane from the factory and the roundabout is called Thornycroft.

Chapter 6

Lincoln
The White Hart Hotel is next to the cathedral in Bailgate. Foster's factory was in Tritton Road (**LN6 7AN**). The site is currently used as a fertiliser store.

Oldbury
The former Metropolitan Carriage and Wagon Works is next to Langley Green Station (**B69 4LZ**), off Tat Bank Road, on the B68. Some of the old factory walls are still there on the site of what was once one of the biggest single factories in the West Midlands. The first TNT plant was close by, off Rood End Road, by the Titford canal.

Bovington/Wool
Off the A352 from Wareham, follow the signs to the Tank Museum (**BH20 6JG**). The proving ground was along the road from the museum to Clouds Hill (last home of T.E. Lawrence). Loading ramps for tanks can be seen at Wool Station (**BH20 6BL**).

Avonmouth/Chittening
From exit 18 on the M5 take the A403. The mustard gas plant was on a site in King's Weston Lane (**BS11**). It was used for a chemical works but is now derelict. The gas was piped for shell filling to Chittening, near Severn Beach. The Shirehampton Yard for horses and mules is close by, alongside the motorway at exit 18.

Chapter 7

Scapa Flow
Kirkwall is north of the Flow and there are ferries to Lyness and Hoxa to the south of the Flow. It is best visited in summer.

Scarborough
The Grand Hotel (**YO11 2ET**) is still the second main landmark (apart from the castle). No. 2 Wykeham Street has been repaired and other bomb sites rebuilt, but the street layout is much as it was on 16 December 1914.

Liverpool Docks
Along Albert Road and Rimrose Road (**L3–L20**).

Sheerness
The dockyard is now an international container terminal, but it is possible to walk round the massive walls. There is a useful heritage centre in Blue Town (**ME12 1RW**). On the way in to the main town there is a fine memorial, including mention of 'citizens' killed in the dockyard explosions.

Chapter 8

Royal Aircraft Establishment, Farnborough
For RAE take exit 4 on the M3, then the A325, which runs alongside the airfield. Hugh Trenchard's office (the man who helped establish the RAF) was in a building (that is still standing) next to the museum and there is a First World War hangar on the edge of the airfield.

Sopwith, Kingston
The offices for the Sopwith (later Hawker) factory are in Canley Park Road, which are now listed buildings. The factory site is now

a development of flats in Canbury Gardens (**KT2 5AU**). The Thames
was used for seaplane trials and is still much as it was then! The RAF
museum in Mill Hill has some very good examples of First World War
aircraft with useful display panels.

Cuffley
The memorial is in East Ridgeway, near the Plough Inn pub (**EN6
4DW**), with a tribute to Lieutenant Leefe Robinson.

Potters Bar
The memorial is in Oakmere Park (**EN6 5JN**). The Zeppelin fell in
Tempest Avenue, named after Lieutenant Tempest, who shot down the
airship.

Chapter 9

RAMC Milbank
The RAMC mess and training centre is now part of the Chelsea College of Art, 57 Milbank, London (**SW1**).

St Mary's Hospital, Paddington
The main entrance is in Praed Street, **W2**. There is a museum of the
work of Alexander Fleming (well worth visiting) and also a fine memorial to the Fifth Army by the main entrance. The museum is on the
floor where Wright, Fleming and the inoculation department worked.

Blackpool
The main training base for the RAMC was on the site of the Blackpool
Victoria Hospital (**FY3 8NR**). There was also a large base in Leeds.

Endell Street
The first hospital in the war to be staffed entirely by women doctors is
in Endell Street, London (**WC2**).

Eastbourne
The site of the rehabilitation hospital was on the western edge of the
town just under the Downs (now housing).

Craiglockhart
Near Edinburgh (**EH14 1DJ**).

Chapter 10

Crewe House
This is now the Saudi Arabian Embassy in Curzon Street (**W1J 5DZ**), but was once owned by the Marquess of Crewe. Gone are the days when every British aristocrat had a magnificent house in Central London.

The Post Office
This was in St Martin's Le Grand (**EC1**). The Telegraph Office was round the corner in Newgate Street, where there is a commemorative plaque inside the BT building. The 5½-acre sorting office was in Regent's Park.

Chapter 11

10 Downing Street
Can be found 150m up from Parliament Square on the left. The buildings are little changed.

The Admiralty
Situated to the right of Horse Guards Parade on Horse Guards Road.

The Ministry of Munitions
Now the Corinthia Hotel, this building (the old Hotel Metropole) is in Northumberland Avenue, near Embankment Station.

Buckingham Palace
At the end of the Mall.

Armistice Day
The possible scorch marks are near the north-west lion by Nelson's Column (closest to Piccadilly).

Bibliography

A Gentleman with a Duster, *The Mirrors of Downing Street*, Mills and Boon, 1920

Amery, L., *My Political Life*, Vol. II, Hutchinson, 1953

Andrew, C., *The Defence of the Realm: The Authorized History of MI5*, Allen Lane, Penguin, 2010

Anon, *Kitchener*, Memorial Book, 1916

Baker-Carr, C.D., *From Chauffeur to Brigadier*, Ernest Benn, 1930

Barnett, C., *The Audit of War: The Illusion and Reality of Britain as a Great Nation*, Macmillan, 1986

Bean, C.E.W., *Official History of Australia in the War of 1914–18*, Vol. III, Angus and Robertson, 1929

Beaverbook, Lord, *Men and Power 1917-18*, Hutchinson, 1956

Beesley, P., *Room 40 British Naval Intelligence 1914-18*, Hamish Hamilton, 1982

Behrend, A., *As from Kemmel Hill: An Adjutant in France and Flanders 1917 and 1918*, Eyre and Spottiswoode, 1963

Bet-El, I.R., *Conscripts: Lost Legions of the Great War*, Sutton, 1999

Blenkinsop, L.J. and Rainey, J.W., *Official History of the War Veterinary Services*, HMSO, 1925

Bone, D.W., *Merchantmen-at-Arms*, Chatto and Windus, 1929

Boraston, J.H. (ed.), *Sir Douglas Haig's Despatches*, Dent, 1979

Bosanquet, N., 'Health Systems in Khaki: The British and American Medical Experience' in Cecil, H. and Liddle, P. (eds), *Facing Armageddon*, Pen and Sword, 1996

Bosanquet, N., 'Lieutenant General A. Sloggett', *Dictionary of National Biography 2002*

Bowser, T., *The Story of British V.A.D. Work in the Great War*, Melrose, 1917

Bragg, L., 'Sound-Ranging', in Bragg, L. et al, *Artillery Survey in the First World War 1914–18*, Field Survey Association, 1971

Brazier, R.H. and Sandford, E., *Birmingham and the Great War 1914–1919*, Cornish Brothers, 1921

Brown, K., *Penicillin Man Alexander Fleming and the Antibiotic Revolution*, Sutton, 2004

Buchan, J., *Memory Hold the Door*, Hodder and Stoughton, 1940

Butler, A.G., *Official History of the Australian Medical Services*, Vol. II, 'The Western Front', Australian War Memorial, 1940

Butler, R., *Richborough Port*, Ramsgate Maritime Museum

Byam, W., *Trench Fever: A Louse-Borne Disease*, London, Henry Froude, 1919

Carlile, J.C. (ed.), *Folkestone During the War 1914-18*, F.J Parsons. n.d.

Chapin, W.A.R., *The Lost Legion*, Springfield Mass., 1926

Chapman-Huston, D. and Rutter, O., *General Sir John Cowans*, Hutchinson, 1924

Chatelle, A., *Calais Pendant La Guerre 1914–18*, Librairie Aristide Quillet, Paris, 1927

Child, J., *The Gallant Company*, Sydney, 1931

Churchill, W.S., *Great Contemporaries*, 1943, Macmillan

Churchill, W.S., *The World Crisis 1916–18*, Part II, Thornton Butterworth, 1927

Clabby, J., *The History of the Royal Army Veterinary Corps 1919–1961*, J.A. Allen, 1963

Clarke, Bob, *Remember Scarborough*, Amberley, 2010

Cocroft W., *Dangerous Energy*, English Heritage, 2000

Cooksley, P., *The Home Front: Civilian Life in World War One*, Tempus, 2006

Coombs, R., *Before Endeavours Fade: After the Battle*, 1976

Crile, G., *An Autobiography*, Philadelphia Lippincott, 1947

Dawson, B., 'The Future of the Medical Profession', in *The Lancet*, 20 July, 1918

Dewar, G.A.B., *The Great Munitions Feat*, Constable, 1921

Donovan, Tom, 'The Chattri', in *Journal of the Indian Military Historical Society*, Summer 2009, Vol. 26, No. 2

Dunn, J.C., *The War the Infantry Knew 1914–19: A Chronicle of Service in France and Belgium*, Jane's, 1967

East Anglia Munitions Comm Stokes W., *A Short History of the East Anglian Munitions Committee in the Great War 1914–18*, n.d.

Edmonds, *Military Operations France and Belgium 1914*, Vol. I, Macmillan, 1922

Egremont, M., *Siegfried Sassoon: A Biography*, Picador, 2005

Elliston, R.A., *Eastbourne's Great War 1914–1918*, SB Publications, 1999

Engineers Royal Work of R.E in the European War 1914–19, 8 Vols, Mackay Chatham, 1922

Evidence of Colonel J.F.C. Fuller in 'Report of the War Office Committee of Enquiry into "Shell Shock"', HMSO, Cmd 1734

Evidence in Ferguson, N., *The Pity of War*, Penguin, 1997

Forester, C.S., *The General*, Penguin, 1956

Foulkes, C.H., *Gas: The Story of the Special Brigade*, Blackwood, 1934

Fuller, J.F.C., *Memoirs of an Unconventional Soldier*, Ivor Nicholson and Watson, 1936

Fulton, J.F., *Harvey Cushing: A Biography*, Charles C. Thomas, 1946

George, M. and C., *Dover and Folkestone During the Great War*, Pen and Sword, 2008

Germains, V.W., *The Kitchener Armies: The Story of a National Achievement*, Peter Davis, 1930

Gladstone, W., *Birds in the Great War*, 1921

Gregory, A., *The Last Great War*, Cambridge University Press, 2008

Grieves, K., *Sir Eric Geddes*, Manchester University Press, 1989

Grigg, J., *Lloyd George From Peace to War 1912–16*, Methuen, 1985

Gwyn, S., *Tapestry of War Harper*, 1992

Haber, L.F., *The Poisonous Cloud*, Oxford University Press, 1986

Haldane, R.B., *An Autobiography*, Hodder and Stoughton, 1929

Halévy, É., *The World Crisis of 1914–18, An Interpretation*, Oxford, 1930

Halpern, P.G., *A Naval History of World War 1*, Naval Institute Press, 1994
Hamilton, J.A.B. *Britain's Railways in World War 1*, Allen and Unwin, 1967
Hankey, Lord, *The Supreme Command 1914–1918*, George Allen and Unwin, 1961
Hanson, N., *First Blitz*, Doubleday, 2008
Harris, K., *Attlee*, Weidenfeld and Nicolson, 1962
Haslam, M.J., 'The Chilwell Story', in *RAOC Gazette*, 1982
Hewison, W.S., *This Great Harbour Scapa Flow*, The Orkney Press, 1985
Hough, R., *Former Naval, Person. Churchill and the War at Sea*, Weidenfeld and Nicolson, 1985
Hunter, G.K., *Light is Messenger: The Life and Science of William Lawrence Bragg*, Oxford University Press, 2004
Hutchinson, W., *The Doctor in War*, Cassell, 1919
Hurd, Archibald, *History of The Great War: The Merchant Navy*, Vol. I, John Murray, 1924
Innes, J.R., *Flash Spotters and Sound Rangers*, George Allen and Unwin, 1935
James, N.D.G., *Gunners at Larkhill*, Gresham Books, 1983
Jellicoe, Viscount, *The Grand Fleet 1914–16*, Cassell, 1919
Jones, H.A., *The War in the Air*, Vol. III, Oxford, 1931
Jones, S. *World War 1 Gas Warfare Tactics and Equipment*, Osprey Publishing, 2007
Jünger, E., *The Storm of Steel*, Chatto and Windus, 1929
Lloyd George, David, *War Memoirs of David Lloyd George*, Ivor Nicholson and Watson, Vol. II, 1933
Ludendorff, E., *War Memoirs*, Longmans, London
Macpherson, W.G., *Medical Services General History*, Vol. I, HMSO, 1921
Macpherson, W.G., et al., *Medical Services Surgery of the War*, HMSO, 1922, Vol. II
Macpherson, W.G., et al., *Medical Services Hygiene of the War*, London, HMSO, 1923
Marder, A.J., *From the Dreadnought to Scapa Flow*, Vol. 1, Pen and Sword, 2013
Marshall, G.C., *My Service in the Great War*, Houghton Mifflin, 1976
Marwick, A., *Women at War*, Fontana/IWM, 1977
McPhail, Helen, *The Long Silence*, Taurus, 1999
Metcalfe P., *The Sailor's War 1914–18*, Blandford Press, 1985
Ministry of Munitions, *Official History*, Vol. VIII, Naval and Military Press reprint
Ministry of National Service, 1917–19, Report, Vol. I, Physical Examination of Men of Military Age by National Service Medical Boards, 1917–18
Mitchell, T.J. and Smith, G.M., *Casualties and Medical Statistics*, HMSO, 1931
MoD: The Old War Office, MoD, 2001
Monash, J., *The Australian Victories in France* in 1918, Hutchinson, n.d.
Morgan, J., *The Secrets of Rue St Roch*, Allen Lane, 2004
Munro, D.J., *Convoys, Blockades and Mystery Towers*, Sampson Low and Marston, 1932
Murray, F., *Women as Army Surgeons*, Hodder and Stoughton, 1920
Newbolt, H., *History of the Great War: Naval Operations*, Vol. V, Longman, 1931
Northover, K., *Banbury During the Great War*, Prospero Publications, 2003
Official History of the Ministry of Munitions, Vol. VIII, Naval and Military Press reprint
Patterson, A., *Temple, Tyrwhitt of the Harwich Force*, Military Book Society, 1973

Peacock, A.D., 'The Louse Problem at the Western Front', in *Journal Royal Army Medical Corps*, Vol. XXVII

Pound, R. and Harmsworth, G., *Northcliffe*, Cassell, 1959

Pratt, E.A., *British Railways and the Great War*, Selwyn and Blount, 1921

Priestley, W.J., *Work of the Royal Engineers in the European War, 1914-1919: The Signal Service in the European War, France*, Mackay, 1921

Prentiss, A., *Chemicals in War*, McGraw-Hill, 1937

Pridham, C.H.B., *Superiority of Fire*, Hutchinson, 1945

Raleigh, W., *The War in the Air*, Vol. I, Oxford, 1922

Richardson, E.H., *British War Dogs*, Skeffington and Son, n.d.

Richter, D., *Chemical Soldiers*, Leo Cooper, 1994

Robertson, W., *From Private to Field Marshal*, Constable, 1921

Robinson, D.H., *The Dangerous Sky: A History of Aviation Medicine*, G.T. Foulis, 1973

Rodman, H., *Yarns of a Kentucky Admiral*, Martin Hopkinson, 1929

Russell, A., *The Machine Gunner*, Roundwood Press, 1977

Ryan, S., *Petain the Soldier*, Yoseloff, 1969

Salter, J.A., *Allied Shipping Control: An Experiment in International Administration*, Oxford University Press

Schreiber, S., *Shock Army of the British Empire*, Praeger/Greenwood, 1997

Scott, W.H., *Leeds in the Great War*, Leeds City Council, 1923

Simkins, P., *Kitchener's Army: The Raising of the New Armies 1914–16*, Pen and Sword, 2007

Smith, Peter J.C., *Zeppelins Over Lancashire*, N. Richardson, 1991

Snowden Gamble, C.F. *The Story of a North Sea Air Station*, Oxford University Press, 1928

Spears, E., *Prelude to Victory*, Heinemann, 1940

Stevenson, D., *With Our Backs To The Wall, Victory and Defeat in 1918*, Allen Lane, 2011

Summerskill, M., *China on the Western Front*, London, 1982

Swinton, E., *Eyewitness*, Hodder and Stoughton, 1932

The Times History of the War, Vols I–XXI, Printing House Square, 1919

The War Cabinet, Report for the Year 1917, Cd 9005, HMSO, 1918

Tuchman, B,. *The Zimmermann Telegram*, Constable, 1959

Vagts, A., *History of Militarism*, Meridian, 1959

Walbrook, H.M., *Hove and the Great War*, The Cliftonviolle Press, 1920

War Office, *Statistics of the Military Effort of the British Empire During the Great War, 1914–20*, London Stamp Exchange

Westman, S., *Surgeon with the Kaiser's Army*, William Kimber, 1968

William Foster and Co., *The Tank, Its Birth and Development*, Wellington Foundry, Lincoln, 1919

Williams, B., *Raising and Training the New Armies*, Constable, 1918

Winter, J. and Robert, J., *Capital Cities at War: London, Paris, Berlin 1914–1919*, Cambridge University Press, 1997

Woodward, D.R. (ed), *The Military Correspondence of Field Marshal Sir William Robertson*, Army Record Society, letter 9 August 1917 to Lt General Sir L.E. Kiggell

Wyeth, R., *The Men of St Mary's and the ANZAC War Graves*, Codford, 2013

Yates, L.K., *The Woman's Part: A Record of Munition Work*, Hodder and Stoughton, 1918

Index